DREAM MACHINES
Porsche

DREAM MACHINES

Porsche

Mike McCarthy

BISON GROUP

First published in 1989 by
Bison Books Ltd
Kimbolton House
117A Fulham Road
London SW3 6RL

ISBN 0-86124-573-3

Printed in Italy

10 9 8 7 6 5 4 3 2 1

Page 1: Classic car, classic face – the current Porsche 911 is still recognizably the same model as that introduced in 1964.

Pages 2-3: One of the greatest racing cars the world has ever seen – the Porsche 956. This is the Jöst-entered car, driven by Wollek and Johansson, at Brands Hatch in 1983.

Below: The way to the future – though the 911 continues, the bulk of Porsche's future sales will come from such models as the 944, here in Turbo form.

Contents

The Porsche Tradition

Ferdinand Anton Porsche was born in 1875 of a Roman Catholic family at Maffersdorf, a town in that most turbulent of political and cultural areas, Bohemia, which at the time was part of the Austro-Hungarian Empire.

He seems to have been a precocious youngster, fitting new-fangled electric lighting to his father's house while still a teenager. He upset his father by going to a technical college, where he received a rudimentary but solid education, rather than joining the family tinsmiths shop.

He served an apprenticeship at an electrical firm in Vienna, and then at 23 years of age joined a company called Lohner. They were carriage-makers turned automobile manufacturers, making electrically-powered machines under license from the French Jeantaud firm: his electrical background thus came in useful.

Two years after joining Lohner, in 1900, when he was just 25 years old, the first of the cars to bear his name appeared: the Lohner-Porsche. Young Porsche's ideas were revolutionary. In the Lohner-Porsche the batteries drove the front wheels via hub-mounted motors.

His next design was yet more brilliant. Since the batteries accounted for most of the weight of electric cars, he did away with them. In 1902 he introduced the Lohner-Porsche *Mixte* system, wherein a petrol engine drove a generator, which in turn drove the wheel-mounted motors.

Even at this stage Porsche was a great racing enthusiast. He competed in both the ordinary electric car and one of the *Mixte* machines, gaining successes with both. In fact the *Mixte* arrangement was exceedingly versatile: during World War One he designed an extremely successful land train for the Austrian army.

In 1905 Porsche was appointed technical head of Austro-Daimler. Here over the years, he was responsible for the Prince Henry model, an air-cooled flat-four aero engine and in 1921 the delightful little Sascha racing car, which achieved some success in the Targa Florio, driven by the legendary Alfred Neubauer. One of his mechanics later became even more famous than either Porsche or Neubauer – we know him today as Marshal Tito.

In 1916 Porsche was appointed Managing Director of Austro-Daimler: he received the Officer's Cross of Franz Joseph for his work on behalf of the war effort; and he was awarded an honorary doctorate by the Technische Hochschule of Vienna.

Long before this Porsche had married Aloisia Johanna Kaes, and had fathered two children – Louise in 1904 and in 1909 Ferdinand Anton Ernst, first nicknamed 'Ferdy,' later altered to 'Ferry.'

By 1923 Dr Porsche, always more interested in matters technical than financial, was at loggerheads with the backers of Austro-Daimler. He comes

Previous pages: Professor Porsche's most prestigious design, the prewar Auto Union.

Above: Ferdinand Anton Porsche.

Left: Ferdinand Porsche (second from right, hands on hips) with the supercharged 1925 2-liter Mercedes.

Above right: Porsche's first design, the Lohner-Porsche, incorporating his patent *Mixte* system of petrol-electric drive.

Right: The *Mixte* system was developed to drive such massive machinery as this World War I 'Land Train.'

Left: This prototype 1932 Porsche Type 12 for Zundapp featured an air-cooled, five-cylinder radial engine on the tail of a back-bone chassis and independent suspension all round. It was a predecessor to the VW Beetle.

Below: Another version of the Type 12, but with Komenda-styled 'streamlined' body. The Beetle gets closer.

Right: While at Daimler-Benz, Porsche instigated the design that eventually led to the magnificent S, SS and, as here, SSK models.

Below right: The Type 32 prototype for NSU, as Type 12 but with a flat four engine. The Beetle's nearly there.

across as a man of blunt manners. This was to lead to many partings of the ways, but in this instance he joined a distant cousin company of Austro-Daimler, the Daimler Motoren Gesellschaft in Stuttgart, as Technical Director. Under his guidance a series of super-charged sports and racing cars began to appear, culminating in the SS, SSK and SSKL machines.

In spite of his prolific output, his time at Daimler was not very happy. A number of factors contributed to this, but probably the most significant was the merger between Daimler and Benz to form Daimler-Benz. Infighting between the two factions broke out, though on the whole it was the Porsche designs that won the day. Matters didn't improve when the Germans wouldn't recognize his honorary Doctorate of Engineering from Vienna — though they hastily re-awarded him the same title from the Stuttgart Technische Hochschule when a Porsche-designed Mercedes won the Targa Florio in 1924.

While he was at Daimler-Benz, incidentally, he came into contact with a car that was to be one of the pointers to the future — the Benz *Tropfenwagen*.

This was the famous Rumpler-designed, teardrop-shaped, mid-engined racer which, though startling to look at, was not successful as it was under-powered. In 1928, when his contract came up for renewal, the company made Porsche an offer calculated to insult: there was no alternative but to leave.

Porsche then moved back to Austria, in 1929, to the Steyr group, as Chief Engineer. He designed for them the small Type 30, taking nine months from initial design to running prototype, and the larger Austria — which featured swing axles at the rear. However, his chair barely had time to become warm when another of those quirks of fate overtook him. Austro-Daimler bought out Steyr! As he was *persona non grata* at Austro-Daimler, they rescinded his three-year contract after only one year. Where next?

All his life Porsche had worked for others, some of whom had made considerably more profit from his designs than he himself. By this time Porsche was 54, and tired of company politics. In spite of a couple of tempting offers,

Porshe decided to set up an independent consulting business, an idea that he had in fact been considering for some time. Thus it was that, by 1931, the Porsche Konstruktionbüro für Motoren-Fahrzeug-Luftfahrzeug und Wasserfahrzeugbau was established. As the name indicates, the company would take on anything that moved on land, sea or in the air, and even such machinery as stationary power plants. Germany in the late 1920s and early 1930s was a difficult place in which to start up a new operation, due to inflation.

The Porsche company's first outside contract, to design a small 2-liter car for the Wanderer concern, was arbitrarily given the project number 'Type 7' — they did not want anyone to think that this was the first from the newly-constituted company! Of much more significance was another early project, the Type 12. The brief came from the Zündapp firm of motorcycle manufacturers; two-wheeler sales were slumping, so the head of Zündapp, Neumeyer, approached Porsche to design for him a small, cheap car that Zündapp could use to bridge the current economic climate.

The Type 12 was decidedly different. For a start the engine was a 1.2-liter five-cylinder radial, water-cooled, mounted at the back of a backbone chassis, with independent suspension all round via transverse leaf springs and semi-leading and trailing arms. It was clothed in a 'streamlined' body.

And then, as production was about to begin, motorcycle sales had started to boom and there was no time and effort at Zündapp to start making cars.

During 1932 Porsche had won another contract, to design yet again a 'small, inexpensive' car for another motorcycle manufacturer, NSU. It was to have a four-cylinder air-cooled engine in the tail, independent suspension all round but this time via torsion bars, and a chassis consisting of a central backbone with sheet metal panels outrigged on either side. Again the mechanicals were enclosed in a steamlined body which bore a striking resemblance to what would later appear as the Volkswagen. The Type 32 could accurately be called the forerunner of the Beetle . . . But, as before, the NSU project was dropped.

Left: The Type 60K10, the VW-based prewar great grandmother of all Porsches, built for a race from Berlin to Rome that never took place.

Below: A young Ferry Porsche (with his wife Dorothea beside him) at the wheel of one of the VW cabriolet prototypes in 1935.

Right: One of the glorious V16 supercharged Auto Union Grand Prix racers.

Below right: The Auto Union's engine position allowed a low frontal area — but imagine putting 600bhp through those narrow tires.

Almost as a sideline, the Porsche company in 1932 had started designing a single seater Grand Prix car for the new formula, which only set a minimum weight limit at 750kg, or about 1650lb. The proposed power plant was a V16 with a novel form of valve gear. It was complex but did work, because from an initial 240 to 250bhp from 4.5 liters, the output rose to no less than 600bhp from 6 liters.

Far more radical, however, was the general layout of the car. The engine was placed amidships with the gearbox behind the rear axle center line. The driver sat in the nose, with the gas tank beween him and the engine. Torsion bar suspension was used; Erwin Komenda's sleek, light bodywork fitted snugly around the mechanicals — and even used doped fabric for some of the panels. The chassis was a tubular affair, the long side members acting also as coolant pipes, taking water from the engine to the front-mounted radiator.

Contrary to popular opinion, Ferry Porsche claims responsibility for the engine location. But, no doubt, the shadow of the Tropfenwagen was lingering somewhere. One reason for the configuration that Ferry Porsche gives is that it optimized the power to weight ratio, though this could be questioned on the grounds that Daimler-Benz achieved similar results with a more conventional layout. Another reason was that, since the gas tank was located at the center of gravity, the handling characteristics of the car stayed constant. This may have been true, but what is equally true is that the handling was constantly tricky as well, and required very brave and incredibly skilled drivers to get the best out of the cars. The mid-engine set up was, of course, to become the standard for all Formula 1 cars some two decades later, but, to be honest, this was more due to the influence of Cooper than Porsche.

Reverting back to 1933, when Hitler announced his grandiose plans for state sponsorship of a Grand Prix car, Daimler-Benz thought they alone would build it. Porsche approached the newly-formed Auto Union combine, the result of a merger between Horch, DKW, Audi and Wanderer and offered them the Type 22. They liked the idea, but there was a condition – that they receive some of the 600,000 mark sponsorship.

In March 1933 Dr Porsche was one of a delegation from Auto Union to Hitler to sell him the Auto Union Grand Prix car. By coincidence Hitler had met Porsche in 1925 at a race meeting at Solitude: Porsche had forgotten, but Hitler had not. The fact that they were both Austrian born may have helped, as would the fact that most of the paperwork had been done. Hitler split the 600,000 marks. The Type 22, the Auto Union GP car, was off and running. Along with Mercedes-Benz they were to dominate prewar racing, much to Hitler's delight.

In January 1934 Hitler opened the Berlin Motor Show, and in his speech propounded the idea of a mass-produced car, simple, reliable, economical, which anyone who could afford a motorcycle could also buy. 'A real people's car – a sort of *Volkswagen*. . . .'

In May that year Hitler and Porsche, along with Hitler's adviser on matters automotive, Jallob Werlin, met again, to thrash out the technical aspects of the Volkswagen. It now appears that the whole Volkswagen concept and organization to go with it were mapped out as well at that meeting.

Since time and money were short, the three prototypes were built in the garage of Porsche's house on Feuerbacher Weg. Once the VW ball was rolling, however, it gathered more and more momentum, albeit in a cumbersome way, so that the program grew rather protracted, and the Porsches at times found life an uphill struggle. For example, a whispering campaign was started to discredit Dr Porsche by pointing out that he was not a Ger-

man, but a Czech. Hitler merely shrugged and, a couple of weeks later, Dr Porsche was told that he and his family were Germans. It was his turn to shrug – there was nothing he could do about it!

As the 1930s drew to a close, Professor Porsche found himself more and more involved in the VW project, designing the Wolfsburg plant and becoming a director of the operation. In spite of this he still had time to concern himself with many of the other Porsche design office schemes and contracts, from a volks-tractor to a multitude of VW variants.

The 1930s also saw the rise of Ferry as a force in the Porsche organization in his own right. Ferry comes across as introvert, shy and shunning publicity, but neverthless a man of strong will. He was *not* going to sit back and bask in his father's glory: he would make his own way in life. Having the Professor as a father was in many ways an advantage, since he could absorb automotive design almost by osmosis – yet it could also be a drawback. For example, there were those who did not or would not believe he was a real engineer: he had to prove otherwise.

His methods were almost the total opposite of his father's. Porsche senior was an intuitive engineer, relying on flair and genius, constantly coming up with new ideas, and almost losing interest in problems once they had been solved. Ferry believed much more in the steady, unspectacular refinement and solid development of an idea to the point where it was more than just feasible or even satisfactory: it had to be absolutely correct from all possible viewpoints.

It is in fact Ferry's philosophy and 'one step at a time to perfection' that has permeated and formed the solid backbone of the Porsche company as we know it today. By following this logical step it is easy to see if the change is actually for the better or worse. Too many changes at once can cloud the potential issues.

Two prewar Porsche projects are worth mentioning at this point. The first was the Type 114. This was to have been a sports-racer, incorporating some astonishing ideas – such as a ten-cylinder engine! This didn't get off the drawing board, but a racing variant of the VW, designated the Type 60K10 and destined for a race that never took place (from Rome to Berlin) did see light of day. If any car could be called the true predecessor of the Porsche, it must be the Type 60K10, for it was based on VW mechanicals suitably modified

Left: The ancestry of the 356 is obvious from the front view of the Type 60K10. The Porsche family, incidentally, used one as everyday transport during the war.

Below: One of the first postwar projects, the Formula 1 Cisitalia, designed for the Italian industrialist Piero Dusio, featured four-wheel drive among other novelties.

Right: The first two prototypes of the 356, with the rear-engined coupe in the foreground and the mid-engined two-seater behind.

with an ultra-sleek coupe body. One look at that car and its layout today and it is obvious whence came the seeds for the 356.

As the war dragged on towards its inevitable – to the Porsches, anyway – conclusion, Stuttgart and its Zuffenhausen suburb came under more and more concentrated attack. The Porsche office was obviously too important to be left there, so the authorities ordered a move to a safe area – Czechoslovakia. Ferry managed to resist this, and eventually found a small sawmill in Gmünd, in Austria, and a glider school at Zell-am-See, close to his farm. By late 1944 the Professor was ill with a gall bladder complaint, and the Porsches were already wondering which of the Allies would take over where in a defeated Germany. As the war ended, the family retreated to Zell-am-See. In the end, the Americans occupied the Zuffenhausen works and Zell-am-See came under their jurisdiction as well. Gmünd fell into the British sector. Because, as German citizens, they were not allowed to hold property, Rabe was put in charge of the Porsche interests at Gmünd and Karl Kern at Stuttgart.

The years between 1945 and 1947 saw the Porsche family at their lowest ebb. Initial Allied interrogations took place at Zell-am-See and Gmünd, and passed off amicably enough.

On 30 July 1945, however, Ferry, Anton Piëch (Ferry's brother-in-law), and other members of the Porsche staff resident at Zell-am-See were arrested and imprisoned. The charges arose from the fact that two dead bodies were found in the house that the Professor used while at Wolfsburg. They were not released until 1 November, by which time they were cleared of any complicity in the murders.

Strangely enough, in spite of his much stronger connections with Wolfsburg, the Professor was not in the groups arrested in July. Instead, in August, he was taken to an old castle near Frankfurt, under 'Operation Dustbin,' an exceedingly odd name for an operation to investigate prominent people. He was not detained for long, as he was obviously so apolitical – a point which Albert Speer made voluntarily to the Allies. On his return he set about obtaining the release of his son and the others, in which he was successful.

And then real disaster stuck. Early that November a Frenchman came calling. He was a representative of Marcel Paul, then Minister of Industrial Production in France. His proposal was to produce a French 'Volkswagen'!

A meeting with the French at Baden-Baden, which included the Professor, Ferry, Dr Piëch and the Professor's nephew Herbert Kaes, took place on 16 November. It was inconclusive, so the family returned to Zell-am-See. Another meeting was called, and the team returned to Baden-Baden. The whole affair seemed to be pie in the sky, so the Professor decided to return to Zell-am-See again on 16 December. The night before they were due to return they were arrested.

The arrest order had been signed by Pierre Teitgen, the Minister of Justice, and there was no love lost between him and Paul, which was probably one of the reasons for the arrests. This whole period is something of a mystery, with only Ferry's account of the affair being anything like extensive. One thing is clear: the French don't come out of it with any distinction.

What appears to have happened is as follows. Elements of the French motor industry heard of Paul's plan for a French 'Volkswagen,' and quite naturally didn't care for it – there was enough competition as it was. So they applied pressure via Teitgen. In addition, Pierre Peugeot brought charges of war crimes against the Professor.

What made these charges so odd was that Peugeot and Porsche had been on amicable terms during the war when the Frenchman's factory had been producing VW parts. In fact, on more than one occasion, Porsche had intervened to *prevent* Gestapo action at Peugeot.

One possible explanation for this about face is that Pierre Peugeot was trying to divert attention from his own wartime activities, a theory to which Ferry subscribes. Whatever the reasons, the Professor was effectively interned, along with Dr Piëch, from the end of 1945 until August 1947. He was, by then, a tired, ill old man.

Ferry, who could show conclusively that he had had no managerial tie-up with VW, had been released over a year earlier, in July 1946. During his and his father's imprisonment up to that point the only working Porsche establishment, at Gmünd, had been run by yet another of the strongwilled Porsche family, Louise Piëch, aided by Karl Rabe. Life for her must have been especially hard, with husband, father and brother in prison.

Demands in Austria just after the war for automotive designs were few and far between. But work for the Porsche company had to be found – and it was. Farm equipment was made and repaired, and soon, too, there was a thriving business in the repair of ex-army VWs – who better to effect these than the company responsible for their design?

At the end of 1946 the Porsches had a stroke of luck. Anton Piëch's secretary had married a Viennese, Karl (later Carlo) Abarth, who had gone to live in Italy. Abarth had met an ex-Porsche employee, Rudolf Hruska, who had been stranded in Italy when the war ended. A correspondence was struck up between Abarth, Hruska and Ferry Porsche, the latter offering the other two Porsche representation in Italy. They jumped at the chance – but what was on offer?

Abarth and Hruska cast about and eventually came into contact with an Italian industrialist, Piero Dusio. He wanted a Grand Prix car: Porsche could design one. A contract was signed. Part of the contract fee, one million francs, was paid as a combination of ransom and bail for the release of the Professor.

The Grand Prix car was highly ambitious, and was to be built under Dusio's Cisitalia car company name. Cisitalia were, at the time, best known for producing little single-seat racing and two-seat sportscars, based mainly on Fiat components.

Left: The chassis of the prototype coupe being built – Ferry Porsche, second from left, looks on. The year is 1948.

Right: One of the first steel-bodied cars, built by Reutter, in 1950.

Below right: September 1984, and Ferry (fourth from left, front) is presented with the special full four-seater 928 on the occasion of his 75th birthday.

The GP car featured a 1.5 liter flat 12 supercharged engine placed (where else?) behind the driver, torsion bar suspension, and the possibility of four wheel drive. Alas only one was to be built, with parts for a few others. It was never raced, for Dusio ran into financial problems.

While the Dusio contract was on the boil, an idea that had been in Ferry's and his father's minds for a long time became firm: to build a sportscar bearing the name of Porsche. On 17 June 1947 a new project number was initiated: the Type 356.

By mid-July preliminary sketches for the Type 356 were ready. They showed a low, slippery, mid-engined roadster, using many VW mechanical parts with a space frame chassis.

In August 1947 Professor Ferdinand Porsche was released by the French. Thus he was in prison when the first of an illustrious marque was conceived.

In the last couple of years of his life Professor Ferdinand Porsche played a part in the fledgling company that rose from the ashes of the prewar concern, but such was his state of health he could really only act in an advisory capacity – which he did, no doubt, to considerable effect. However, in November 1950, he suffered a stroke from which he never recovered, and died in January 1951.

If the 1930s were the time of Ferry's effective apprenticeship for greater things, the 1940s saw him mature into a true leader, and the 1950s were to be perhaps his greatest period. Luck, reputation, contacts, all played a part in the rise of Porsche, but in those early days it was Ferry's business instinct and careful technical approach that had as much, if not more, effect. Remember, too, that Porsche were not just trying to break into motor manufacturing but were carrying on with the traditional Porsche research, design and development business as well.

Two external contracts stand out. The first arose in 1952, when the Porsche importer in America, the great entrepreneur Max Hoffman, arranged a meeting between Ferry and the management of Studebaker, the intention being that Porsche would become consultants to the South Bend, Indiana, company. An agreement was reached whereby Porsche would carry out feasibility studies on a front engined (air or water cooled, V8) car with rear wheel drive. Ferry wanted something smaller, with a rear engine naturally, but nothing came of this – until, years later, the Chevrolet Corvair appeared. However, Studebaker ran into financial difficulties, and, as with many Porsche projects, nothing was to come of their efforts.

The second contract was probably one of the most important that the Porsches ever signed. Against all predictions, VW had risen like the proverbial phoenix from the desolate remains of Hitler's one-time wonder factory. Helped at first by the British, a trickle of cars began to run off the assembly lines. And then a brilliant businessman, Heinz Nordhoff, an ex-Opel employee, took charge, and the miracle of the Beetle happened. By 1948 they were well on their way to being Germany's biggest car maker. In September of that year Porsche assumed a position they had held before the war: consultants to VW. This not only brought in an immediate cash payment, but royalties on every Beetle too. It was a financial injection that was a godsend to Porsche. In return Porsche agreed not to design a competitive car for any other manufacturer. In addition, Porsche would be responsible for VW in Austria, the Piëch side of the family looking after this business, later to become famous as Porsche-Salzburg.

All through the 1950s Porsche concentrated on one basic model, the 356, gradually developing, refining, and perfecting it in accord with Ferry's philosophy. It was a time of steadiness, growth and stability. There were but two equal partners in 'Dr. Ing. h.c. F. Porsche K.G.', Ferry and Louise.

In the late 1950s the third generation of Porsches appeared on the scene (Ferry had four sons, Louise three and a daughter.) Ferry's eldest, Ferdinand Alexander ('Butzi') joined the company in 1957, and by 1961 was head of the styling department. His grandfather was a technical genius, his father, organizational; Butzi turned out to be the artistic member of the family. To him goes the credit of one of the most timeless shapes ever: the 911.

In 1961, too, another Ferdinand, this time a Piëch and Louise's eldest son, joined the company. If anything he was very much in his grandfather's mold, displaying a remarkable engineering aptitude. He swiftly took in hand the flat 6 engine that appeared in Butzi's 911. He was also responsible for one of Porsche's other all-time greats, the 917. Peter Porsche, Butzi's younger brother, also joined in 1963, to become the head of production in 1965. Finally Michael Piëch joined in 1971 – but for less than a year.

In fact 1971 was a traumatic year for the Porsche and Piëch families. It had gradually become clear over the preceding few years that an internal battle was going on between the two branches of the family. This was bad for both and, more importantly, the company too could suffer. On top of that, with the Porsches and Piëches filling the top slots, ambitious outsiders saw little possibility of advancement, while there was always the danger that non-family members of the company would give in to family member decisions, whether they were right or not.

The cure was stunningly drastic. Ferry called a family conference in June 1971 to discuss these matters. There was really only one answer: *no* member of either family could hold a management position without the agreement of all the others – an unlikely event.

Thus the Porsche dynasty broke up. Ferry stayed on with the titular title of Chairman of the Board of Directors. Butzi started his own studios, Porsche Design, now a well-established firm whose products include the famous matt-black watch and dark glasses. Ferdinand Piëch is head of Audi engineering, and has such masterpieces as the quattro to his credit.

But the Porsches we see on the roads today still have a family connection. They stand for all that is best in automotive engineering, a quality instilled into the company by that greatest of geniuses, Ferdinand Porsche.

The Die is Cast

By early 1948, the wooden sawmill at Gmünd saw a bodyless chassis drive off for testing: behind the wheel was Ferry Porsche himself. The Type 356 was rolling.

Unlike future road cars, that original 356 had a tubular space frame chassis. Another break from what was to become Porsche road car tradition was that the VW engine and transmission were reversed, with the power unit ahead of the rear axle and the transmission trailing behind. This also necessitated turning the VW rear suspension through 180°, so that the torsion bars were right in the tail. At the front standard VW suspension was fitted – twin trailing arms each side with cross tubes between them carrying the torsion bars. A mildly tuned VW 1131cc engine was used, though an increase in compression ratio from 5.8:1 to 7:1 was rather bold considering the poor quality of fuel then available.

With about 40bhp on tap, this ultra-light test chassis survived the early tests, and was then clothed with a svelte, light, open two-seater body, designed by Erwin Komenda to Ferry's specifications. The actual fabrication of the aluminum body was by a skilled panel beater, Friedrich Weber, who had the habit of disappearing every so often to imbibe a little, after which his workmanship declined: the body took a little longer than expected to make, but Weber was indispensable.

Concurrently with the open two-seater, a coupe model was being designed, the 356/2, and it was the first four of these that a Swiss, von Senger, ordered, sight unseen.

For the coupes, Ferry and Rabe reverted to the standard VW, soon to be Porsche, layout, with the engine slung behind the rear axle. There were two reasons for this. The first was that the rearward placing of the torsion tubes at the back placed stresses in the out-rigged chassis tubing that were unwelcome – one of the struts had indeed broken on trial. The second was that, with the coupe bodywork, the engine took up the space behind the seats which could be usefully used for luggage. Other reasons were that, with the engine further away, the car would be quieter, and no fundamental change to the transmission was required for the 180 degree reversal.

Once again Komenda designed the light alloy bodywork, but this time it enveloped a sheet steel chassis, consisting of a platform with side sills and a longitudinal tunnel fronted by a boxed-scuttle-cum footwell and a fabricated section behind to take the power train and suspension. The definitive 356 basics had at last appeared.

Naturally, the engine was the VW boxer unit. Some of the first 356s were made with the standard 1131cc capacity (the first publicity brochures give this figure) but pretty soon the bore was reduced slightly, from 75mm to 73.5mm, to give a capacity of 1086cc – a figure compatible with the then-popular 1100cc class in motor racing.

That first coupe saw the light of day in August 1948, like the prototype being tested in chassis form. Gradually a trickle of cars started appearing from Gmünd – but it really was a trickle, for parts were hard to come by, and at times whatever was available would be fitted – hence, for example, the variations in engine capacity. Secondly Gmünd was way off the beaten track. Thirdly, though orders were coming in, from Holland and Portugal for example, actually obtaining permits to import Austrian-built cars into those countries was very difficult: the Dutch order was cancelled for this reason, while the Portuguese suggested an exchange of sardines for cars! Then, too, the Austrian Schilling was not regarded as hard currency, so obtaining parts from other countries including Germany was almost impossible – though von Senger helped by sending VW parts to Gmünd via Switzerland, which he could do as a Swiss national and as agent for VW in Switzerland.

Previous pages: One of the most famous Porsches of all time, the ugly but effective Speedster. Because of its lack of trim it was very light and thus very quick, and was highly popular on the race tracks.

Below left: The prototype mid-engined 356 roadster being demonstrated at Laguna Seca in America in the eighties.

Bottom left: The original mid-engined concept was deemed impractical because of the difficulty of getting at the engine and a lack of passenger space but it allowed a lovely, pure shape.

Right: The interior trim was exceedingly basic but, for its day, the cockpit was very spacious.

Below: One of the first public displays of the 356, at the Geneva Motor Show in 1950 – note the curved quarter windows, indicating a Gmünd-built car.

Left: One of the very early coupes, registered in Britain, with the bumper attached to the body.

Below left: By 1964 bumpers had been strengthened, headlamps raised and, in this particular example, there was a ferocious engine under the bonnet, indicated by a 'Carrera' badge.

Below: An alternative body style to the coupe was the cabriolet, here seen on a 1951 356.

The Gmünd-built coupes were quite distinctive: apart from the two-piece windshield they had small, curved three-quarter lights in the side windows. And one of the Gmünd coupes holds a very special place in Porsche history: it was the first works entry in a major international race.

By 1949, it was obvious that Gmünd was no place to make cars: but the works in Zuffenhausen still stood, occupied by the Americans. Initial approaches for the return of the property was made through the mayor of Stuttgart, a Dr Klett. It looked as if the Porsches could have their premises back by mid to late 1950. Ferry Porsche asked an old friend, Albert Prinzing, to oversee the transfer to Germany. To keep matters ticking over there, a group of technicians was sent from Gmünd. Since there was no way they could use the works, they opened shop in the garage in the Porsche home in Feuerbacher Weg.

Obviously 'production' could not take place in such cramped conditions, even after appropriating the cook's room. In addition, rent from the Americans and royalties from VW meant that cash was accumulating, which would be highly taxable unless it was offset against a business. A restart in Germany was becoming imperative. Fortunately just down the road from the Zuffenhausen works were Reutter, the coachbuilders. Porsche took over a part of their factory to make the 356 chassis, while Reutter themselves made the bodies.

At this time, the Porsche management foresaw a maximum number of sales, world-wide, of 500 cars — how naive this seems in retrospect. However, even this number meant at least one fundamental change: the bodies would have to be made of steel, not aluminum, since the latter was in short supply and did not really lend itself to mass production at Reutters, even in such limited numbers. Komenda and the others took the opportunity to incorporate modifications too. The windshield, for example, was lowered,

widened and curved at the edges so that the distinctive Gmünd quarter lights were deleted. On Good Friday, 1950, the first German-built Porsche rolled out of Reutter's establishment.

To finance the operation, there were the VW royalties and the American's rent, but more was needed. Prinzing toured the German VW dealers and came back with firm orders for 37 cars. 500 cars world-wide? By March 1951 they had made 500, and the 1000th was completed by August that year.

Those first Zuffenhausen Porsches retained many of the VW engine components, but the rest of the design was becoming more and more Porsche. There were special heads, for example, that overcame the Beetle's asthmatic breathing. With 40bhp on tap, the little low streamlined coupes could exceed 80mph quite easily, and soon private owners were entering sporting events. They were helped quite considerably at the Frankfurt Show in April 1951, where the big news was the introduction of a new engine. It had a capacity of 1300cc and produced 44bhp at 4200rpm.

That wasn't the end of the engine story that year, though. In October at the Paris Salon one of the two cars displayed, 'still liberally smeared with dead flies and dirt' as John Bolster of *Autosport* put it, was a Gmünd coupe with an even bigger 1500cc engine tucked in its tail.

It was the 1300s and 1500s that were produced in greatest quantities, and that could truly be said to have put Porsche on the map. Following Ferry's guidelines, improvements were phased in as and when they had been tested and approved, although as the historian Karl Ludvigsen says, 'in the first two and a half years at Zuffenhausen Porsche made almost as many alterations as automobiles!'

The expected return of the Porsche works in 1950 was prevented by the Korean war. A wooden prefabricated barrack block was bought in late 1950 to house the administration and design staff, but production at Reutter was

severely hampered by sheer lack of space. A new factory was desperately needed: the Studebaker contract provided the necessary capital, land was bought behind the Reutter factory, and by the end of 1952 production of 356s was under way. It wasn't until 1 December 1955, that the original Porsche works were returned to the Porsches by the Americans – exactly 25 years from the date of the founding of the company.

The majority of Porsches were either coupes or the open cabriolets. In mid-1952 the bumpers were moved away from the body, and a one-piece windshield replaced the divided one. At the same time the limitations of the VW gearbox became more and more obvious. There was the lack of synchromesh for a start: crash changes were alright for experts, but as less experienced mortals bought Porsches, so complaints increased. In addition, of course, the transaxle had been designed for puny VW outputs, not the 70bhp of the 1500. Porsche had already designed new internals incorporating their own patented balk ring synchromesh system, for VW – and had it turned down. But the design was there: Porsche found a company, Getrag, to build the new transaxle for them. To solve some of the initial teething problems a newcomer was assigned to the job, a youngster called Helmuth Bott. The Paris Salon in 1952 thus saw the near-definitive 356.

Continuing with the main volume-produced models, the 356 design stayed relatively stable until 1955. In September 1955 a whole raft of changes were introduced. So many, that a new designation, the 356A was coined. These included an increase in capacity, from 1.5 to 1.6 liters (1582cc as against 1488cc): the suspension was modified to reduce the oversteering characteristics; and wheel diameters were made smaller (from 16in to 15in) and rim widths wider.

There were, however, a number of variations, at least a couple of which were to join the ranks of the greatest Porches ever. The first was to be the inimitable Speedster.

The Speedster was really the brain-child of the ebullient Max Hoffman, Porsche's East Coast American distributor. Like the Porsches he was an Austrian by birth, and was a friend of the family. He had cashed in on the post-war sportscar boom in America via showrooms in Park Avenue in New York. Ferry thought there was a market in the States for a handful per year, but Hoffman replied that that was how many he wanted per week!

The predecessor of the Speedster came in the middle of 1952 when Porsche produced a very small run of a model called the America Roadster. These were stripped two-seaters, very light, intended mainly for racing. Their body style aft of the windshield was unusual, too, with cutaways in the doors and humped rear fenders in place of the usual Porsche flowing line: Hoffman thought the standard Porsche 'looked funny,' and this was one of Porsche's design suggestions for a more state-of-the-art shape. Considering its scarcity the America Roadster won an inordinate number of races in the hands of such as Phil Walters, Briggs Cunningham, John Bentley, Jack McAfee and the husband and wife team of John and Josie von Neumann.

By 1954 Hoffman was pressing for a 'cheap' Porsche. The team at Zuffenhausen resurrected the America Roadster design but the basis was the cabriolet, since it had the strengthening necessary for a convertible. On to this Beuttler grafted a two-seater body of quite astonishing proportions: the most common comparison was of an inverted bathtub. A miniscule windshield cut down dramatically on frontal area, but the hood that went with it removed almost all vision except directly forward. The interior trim was pared down to the minimum. Max Hoffman received his 'cheap' Porsche, in September 1954.

Because it was so light, the Speedster promptly became the darling of the race track. To this day it is one of Porsche's great cult cars.

Another design that would be an all time great was named after the gruelling race that ran the length of Mexico, the Carrera Panamericana, in which

Above left and right: With its dumpy body and miniscule windshield, the Speedster is often compared to an inverted bath tub. With the soft top up, vision out is almost negligible, but it means very little frontal area for additional performance. Ugly, maybe – but the Speedster is now highly collectable.

Right: Like all 356s, the majority of the engine is hidden down in a deep, dark bay, but most vital items requiring regular attention are reasonably accessible, as demonstrated by this 1959 356A coupe.

Left: Towards the end of its life – this is a 1964 Carrera 2 – the 356 was a refined, sophisticated and much more powerful machine.

Below left: The author conducting a lovely 1956 'Damen' Cabriolet for a feature in *Classic and Sportscar* – he found it a highly civilized, highly enjoyable, jewel of a machine.

Right: One of the Porsche's less splendid ideas was routing the exhaust pipes through the rear bumper over-riders.

Below: A 365B Cabriolet, one of the few convertibles that looks good with its hood raised.

Porsche had distinguished themselves. In particular a special racer, the Type 550 (of which more later) had walked away with the 1500cc class in 1954, powered by an engine which made its first official public appearance at Paris in October 1953.

This engine was something special. It was the brainchild of Ernst Fuhrmann who had worked on the Cisitalia project and had previously designed a special camshaft for racing. It featured no less than four camshafts, two per bank, driven by shafts and bevel gears. Apart from this unusual valve train, the engine featured twin plugs per cylinder and a roller bearing crankshaft. Its quoted output was 110bhp at 7000rpm. It was not really intended to be a road-going engine, but . . .

Thus one of the sensations of the Frankfurt Show in September 1955 was the Carrera – the marriage of the 356 body and most of its running gear with the four-cam engine. The Carrera, like most other Porsches, would have a long and distinguished competition career, first in 1500, then in 1600, and finally in 2000cc form, by which time it was known as the Carrera 2 and had a top speed around the 130mph mark. In spite of a racing-orientated engine it was a tractable road car, but didn't really take kindly to low speed running.

This was unfortunate for those who had brought the car for its glamour – changing the plugs, all eight of them, was a long, costly and finger nail breaking operation. The ultimate development of the 356 Carrera was a light-weight, the GTL, better known as the Abarth-Carrera.

In fact the car should perhaps be better known as the Zagato-Carrera, for it was this Italian coach-builder whose designer, Franco Scaglione, produced the drawings for the shape while Zagato produced the actual aluminum bodies. Since Zagato also provided bodies for Porsche competitors such as Alfa Romeo, it was perhaps felt politically wise for Porsche's old friend Carlo Abarth to act as front man for the tie-up: hence the name. In 1963 yet another variant of the 356 Carrera appeared, this time with a Butzi Porsche-designed body: it had a competition life of but one year, in which it was reasonably successful, and only two were built.

Reverting to the production models, 1956 saw the 10,000th Porsche roll off the lines. While 1957 saw the 1300cc engines finally dropped, diaphragm clutches first appeared – and the exhaust pipes on the pushrod engines were routed through the fender overriders. This was intended to give better ramp clearance, but merely resulted in dirtying the overriders and causing problems when the tips of the pipes rusted. Not all of Porsche's ideas were 100 percent brilliant.

The Speedster was dropped too – much to the vocal chagrin of its adherents. Yet it had never been a big seller, and as it was trimmed to the bone to bring costs down, its profit margin was minimal. In 1958 it was replaced by the Speedster D (named after its body-builder Drauz), which was more luxuriously equipped and had a 'proper' windshield. You could even see out of it with the roof up, but the purists sneered. The name was hastily revised to the Convertible D so Speedster fanatics wouldn't be too upset.

The next few years saw steady refinement of the 356 theme, though with relatively few dramatic changes, apart from the introduction of the 356B in September 1959. The most startling was a new nose, with raised headlamps and higher, more prominent bumpers at either end. Traditionalists didn't really take to the, quite literal, facelift, but in fact it portended the shape of things to come, for there was a hint of the 911 in the lines. A new gearbox allowed the rear seats to be dropped for more headroom.

From 1958 on, only the 1600 engine was offered (Carreras apart), but in 1960 another unit was added. The cars fitted with it were called Super 90s, from the quoted output of the engine. Under the skin, too, other significant changes were incorporated in the Super 90: Koni dampers all round, and the

Left: One of the rarest, and certainly most desirable, of all the 356 variants was the Abarth-Carrera, a production 356B Carrera under its Zagato-designed and built all-aluminum body. Only 20 were made.

Right: Future World Champion Jim Clark started his racing career in a 356 in Scotland.

Below: Top of the standard 356 range (excluding the Carrera) in 1959 was the Super 90, here in Cabriolet form. The additional luggage rack sits uneasily on the tail of this otherwise superb example.

Ausgleichfeder, a compensating spring, at the rear. This was a single, wide leaf spring joined to the suspension either side: it acted in the opposite sense to an anti-roll bar, thus reducing rear roll stiffness and forcing the front suspension to take a greater share of the cornering loads and hence increasing understeer. Another innovation was the adoption of radial ply tires, but only after Porsche and Dunlop had cooperated closely to arrive at a specification that was acceptable to Porsche.

The early 1960s were the golden years of the 356 series. The range of body styles was the widest ever, with Reutter making the coupes and cabriolets, Zagato making the Abarth-Carreras, Drauz (and for a brief while D'Ieteren Frères) making the two-seater Roadsters, and Karmann the Hardtop-Coupe which, as its name suggests, was the cabriolet with a fixed roof.

Part of the reason for the diversification of suppliers was the ever-increasing production rate which was taxing the Reutter works. In 1960 the company produced 7598 cars, in 1961 7664, in 1962 some 8205, and in 1963 a total of 9672.

In 1961 another important step in Porsche history was taken: the construction of the company's new proving ground at Weissach was started. This was to grow eventually into a massive complex which could put all cars, from secret prototypes for large manufacturers to Porsche's own 917s, through their paces.

That same year saw the last of the major changes to the 356 body shell. The most obvious differences were the considerably increased glass area at front and back and twin air intakes on the rear deck. In an effort to obtain more luggage space the area under the trunk opening was completely rearranged, the gas tank being flattened and spread out, with the filler in the front wing instead of being inside the trunk.

Come 1963 the end was in sight for the 356 – from that year on the new 911 would begin to dominate. But there was still life in the old model, and in September, at the Frankfurt Show, the 356C was introduced. The major change here was the introduction of disk brakes for the first time on production Porsches. Never one to accept other people's designs if they thought they could do better, Porsche had been trying to make their own for years, but costs always worked against them. Thus it was that for the 356C Alfred Teves, under their trade name of Ate, provided the braking system – but Porsche insisted on incorporating at least one of their developments: the handbrake operated on small drums within the rear disks. With the 356C, too, the engine range was simplified even further: the 1600 standard was dropped, the 1600S or 'Super 75' as it had been briefly called became the 1600C, and the Super 90 became the 1600SC.

In 1963, too, Porsche bought out the body building side of Reutter including the factory in which they had started by renting a small corner. The part of the business they did not acquire was renamed and soon became famous as Recaro, the seat manufacturers.

After producing 16,668 of the Type 356Cs, the last of the model came off the assembly line in 1965. For a car whose originators envisaged a maximum of 500 sales, the Type 356 had become a phenomenon. When the last car rolled away, it was the 76,303rd of the model. . . .

The Great Survivor

The second generation of the Porsche dynasty and genius, in the person of Ferry, showed its ability through the Type 356. For its successor, the 911 series, the third generation proved that none of the family traditions were being diluted: on the contrary, for two of the Professor's grandchildren, Butzi Porsche and Ferdinand Piëch, were to play vital roles in its success, while Ferry still took the guiding hand as his father had done before.

By the late 1950s the 356 was an established success, and as we have seen, more were produced in the last few years of its life than ever before. But from an ultra-light, super-smooth, rather spartan little GT it had, over the years, put on weight, become more luxurious, required ever more powerful engines to maintain its speed, and of course its price had put it in the realms of the upper end of the sportscar market. It had never been cheap: when first introduced into America it cost more than a Cadillac convertible or an XK120.

Quality and engineering were the 356's plus points, but over the years some of the very factors that made it so successful began to appear as drawbacks as Porsche ownership increased. The lack of space for people and luggage became a growing criticism. The handling, too, was a bone of contention: drivers either loved it or hated it. Porsche's engineers had, by constant development, managed to keep one step ahead of downright condemnation. And what had been a startling speed capability in the early years (regardless of engine size) was beginning to look, if not humdrum, then nothing particularly special, as more ordinary and cheaper cars caught up.

So it was that in 1959 Ferry Porsche gave the engineering team the go-ahead for a new type of Porsche.

By 1959 Butzi Porsche was in charge of Porsche styling, and he began exploratory work on one of the most important facets of the new car, the shape. There was one major prerequisite: it had to *look* like a Porsche; lineality had to be maintained.

By 1962, however, there had been a fundamental change of attitude: the new car was to be a 2 + 2, not a full four-seater. Ferry had decided to leave such machines and their attendant bulk to the establishment: Mercedes-Benz and BMW. 'Shoemaker, stick to your last' was the way he put it. The wheelbase was brought down to a little over 4in more than that of the 356. Butzi kept the bottom half of a design that he had already evolved, adding a sleeker, slimmer roofline that retained the spirit of Komenda's 356 coupe design, but with considerably more glass area. This was the shape that was finally adopted, that was and still is one of the most beautiful and distinctive ever seen. And it *looked* like a Porsche.

While the body concept was being developed, two other areas came in for consideration. The first was the engine and transmission, the second the suspension. Again a 'clean sheet' approach was adopted.

Porsche's engine experience had revolved around pushrod fours, four overhead cam fours (in the Carrera), and four overhead cam eights (in racing). A lot of work had gone into the four, but it was not powerful enough for the bigger, heavier new model: the eights were powerful but complex. So a compromise was reached: a six-cylinder unit. Naturally it was to be air-cooled, and naturally it was to be sited in the tail. No other configuration was seriously considered. The man in charge of engine development was Ferdinand Piëch.

In the meantime work on the chassis/substructure was in hand. Komenda at first stuck to his guns that the new car should be a four-seater, but when Ferry asked Reutter to design the underpinnings for a 2 + 2 he gave in gracefully and cooperated fully. The result was a monocoque unit, not dissimilar to that of the 356, clothed in Butzi's body style.

The running gear of the new car represented yet another break with Porsche tradition. Gone were the transverse torsion bars and trailing arms at the front, and swing axles at the rear.

Space was needed up front: the 356 set up took up too much. There was an elegant solution that other manufacturers had successfully adopted: MacPherson struts, first used by Ford in the early 1950s. Instead of the usual coil spring arrangement, however, the Porsche engineers couldn't resist retaining torsion bars. They did so in a way that gave them yet more luggage space, and was neat and effective at the same time: they incorporated them into the lower wishbones.

At the rear a semi-trailing arm arrangement was used, with transverse torsion bars as the springing medium.

To complete the specification, steering was by rack and pinion, disk brakes were used at each corner, and a five-speed gearbox was situated in the standard Porsche position, ahead of the engine and axle center line.

All this, then, was the basic configuration that appeared on a car, given the type number 901, that made its sensational debut at the Frankfurt Motor Show in September 1963. It is still the quintessential configuration that survives to this day, though it is probable that no single part has remained exactly as it was on that prototype. Nevertheless the layout, body shape, the flat boxer engine and suspension have remained constant in concept if not in execution.

The 901 on show at Frankfurt in 1963 was, however, just a tempter, for production would not get under way until nearly a year later. When it did start trickling off the assembly lines one problem cropped up almost immediately – one that Porsche could not have foreseen, and one which must have annoyed Ferry Porsche in particular. Peugeot, a company whose head had played such a depressing part in the imprisonment of Professor Ferdinand, objected to the name, claiming (as, under French law, they had a perfectly

Previous pages: The classic early 911, in this case a 1967 short-wheelbase S on the famous five-spoke forged aluminum wheels.

Left and right: The license plate says it all – this is one of the prototype 911s, before the argument with Peugeot which saw the name change to 911. The lovely, clean Butzi Porsche-penned lines of the early 911s are arguably best seen from this rear three-quarter view.

Above right: Over the years those original, simple, lines have been modified more than somewhat as this line-up of later models at a Porsche Club meeting indicates.

Left: Extremes of the 911 range, with a smooth-running, roadable Targa in the foreground and the stunning semi-racer Carrera 2.7 behind.

Below: The 1975 non-turbo range, with two body styles, Targa and Coupe, and two engines, 2.7 and 3.0 liters.

Right: Almost from the start of 911 production more powerful 911s appeared on the scene. This 1965 S with the optional alloy wheels and 'Porsche' logo decals on the side was one of them.

legal right to) that they had cornered the market in car designations which included three numbers with a central zero (as in 104, 302, 505 and so on). This rather ignored the fact that Bristol had been making 40-cars for years, and a Porsche 904 had been running on the race tracks, so Porsche might just have a prior claim to 90-numbers. However 901 was not fully established, so Porsche simply changed the name to 911.

Thus 1964 saw the 911 enter into production, alongside the 356 initially, but at the end of 1965 the latter was finally phased out altogether.

There were, of course, teething troubles. One in particular involved the old Porsche bug-bear, handling. When the 911 appeared it was on relatively narrow tires and the weight of the engine was higher than expected. In addition the Porsche engineers were learning about the problems that can arise when MacPherson strut suspension is in volume production, as distinct from careful assembly in laboratory conditions. They were far from alone — most manufacturers who adopt this system have found themselves baffled at some time.

The net result was that the early cars understeered quite considerably under moderate cornering loads but would flick into the dreaded oversteer if the driver lifted off at high cornering speeds. In addition straight line stability was not all it should have been, and some cars had different characteristics depending on whether or not they were turning left or right! To achieve consistency, Ing. Tomala, who had succeeded Karl Rabe as Technical Director in 1962, specified incredibly close tolerances and a complex production technique. Neither really worked, and at least one odd solution, involving lumps of iron in the corners of the front fenders which affected both weight distribution and polar moment of inertia, was tried. Suspension development was in fact almost continuous, and when Ing. Tomala left Ferdinand Piëch took over as head of development. Under his rule the defects were gradually ironed out. One of the first changes came in early 1966, with a switch from Solex to Weber carburettors to overcome a flat spot. But the real news came in August.

Firstly there was an S version, with power up to 160bhp, giving a top speed of 140mph as against the standard car's 130mph. To go with the added performance came ventilated disk brakes, clearly visible behind meaty five-spoke forged alloy wheels, their pattern almost becoming a hallmark of Porsches for years to come.

Secondly, a brand new bodyshell also appeared that month. It was basically a convertible but incorporated a hefty roll-over bar or hoop. Like the Carrera before it, it was named the Targa after a famous race with strong Porsche connections, the Targa Florio.

Butzi, who had designed the Targa, wanted a fully opening convertible, but impending American regulations seemed to indicate at the time that such an arrangement would not meet roll-over requirements. He also wanted special panel work for the tail, but this was ruled out on cost grounds. Most importantly, however, was the fact that when the roof is chopped off a monocoque structure it is weakened considerably, and strengthening the base structure often adds more weight than the removal of the top. The hoop solved these problems.

Having come to the conclusion that the hoop was essential, Porsche turned what might have been an unacceptable feature into a novelty with such success that other manufacturers soon followed, and the generic term 'targa top' passed into motoring language. And unlike the proliferation of bodyshells that abounded with the 356, the 911 would retain but two, the coupe and the Targa, until 1982 and the appearance of the Cabriolet.

In 1967 Porsche decided to offer an automatic transmission, and the 'Sportmatic' gearbox appeared. This was in fact more 'sport' than 'auto-matic,' since it consisted of a normal four-speed transmission, but with a tor-que converter and a clutch as well. A switch in the gear lever knob caused the clutch to disengage, thus dispensing with the clutch pedal but leaving the driver still to change gear.

The first major revisions to the range came in August 1968, with the B Series. The most important of these was the extension of the wheelbase by just over two inches. This was achieved by moving the rear wheels (and wheelarches to disguise the change) back, but leaving everything else where it was. To accommodate the new angle of the drive shafts, Löbro units incorporating Rzeppa constant velocity joints were used, and the semi-trailing arms were lengthened.

The purpose behind these changes was to try and equalize the weight distribution a little more, and thus help out in the handling department. Magnesium replaced aluminum for the crankcase and twin batteries were mounted up front, improving matters even further. For the most powerful S versions, rim widths were increased to six inches. The result hoped for was achieved —

Left: The Targa was Butzi Porsche's attempt to make an open Porsche that would meet impending legislation in America on roll-over protection. It was so successful that the term 'Targa' is now generic for this type of body.

Below left: This 1969 911E looks original but has been fitted with a later front spoiler.

Right: This early Targa has also been modified with the fitment of one of the enormous rear spoilers from a Turbo.

Below: An early 911E – compare the original slender bumpers of the pre-1974 models with those of the later cars such as the Targa on the opposite page.

the understeer was reduced at low cornering speeds and the oversteer reduced at high speeds.

For the 1969 model year, Bosch mechanical fuel injection was adopted, another significant first for production Porsches, which helped considerably towards the reduction in emissions, something which was giving automotive engineers throughout the world headaches as the American clean-air lobbyists tightened the thumbscrews. The E version also received Boge self-leveling struts at the front in place of the usual dampers as a way of improving the quality of the ride. The objective was perhaps laudable, but the units were costly and their effect on handling was questioned. Like the Sport-

matic transmission, this was one alteration that was not universally accepted. The S, too, was equipped with the fuel injection system, pushing power up to 170bhp at 5500rpm.

As night follows day, the C and D series followed the B for the 1970 and 1971 model years. The significant modification was the first of the increases in engine capacity, from 1991cc to 2195cc. The reason for this was to increase bottom end torque and thus driveability, notably for the American market which put great store on low speed lugging, even in Porsches.

But the 2.2-liter engine was only a brief stepping stone to the next in the series, the E and F models, which expanded capacity to 2.4 liters (actually 2341cc) via a longer stroke. At the same time, however, the compression ratio was reduced, so that the engines would run on low-lead fuel – emissions were playing an ever dominant part at this time. As power and torque had risen quite considerably since the original 2-liter was introduced, a new transmission appeared on the scene: this reversed the pattern of the previous box, putting fifth out on a limb instead of first, an arrangement that made town driving easier.

The first tentative steps towards the use of aerodynamics came in the form of an air dam under the nose of the 911S in 1972: the next year it was fitted to all models.

Thus the development for the 911 series was being set: a little bit here, a little bit there. A gradual increase in engine capacity; wider wheels and tires to take advantage of rapidly moving technology in the tire industry; the idea that aerodynamic lessons learnt on the track could be applied to road cars; the increasing importance of emission control and safety regulations – all these factors were influential.

But if progress on the technical side was following a logical sequence, other matters weren't. Production in 1969 was 15,275 cars, in 1970 it was up to 16,761 cars. In 1971, however, inflation hit the industry world-wide, the Deutsche-mark-to-dollar rate worsened, and Porsche faced the indignity of a three-week strike, the first ever in their history. Sales fell to a disastrous 11,715 . . .

On top of that the Porsche/Piëch battle was coming to a climax. When Ferry, Louise and the rest of the family made that momentous decision not to allow individual members to hold elevated positions in the company, Heinz Branitski took over as financial director, Helmuth Bott was placed in charge of development, Anatole Lapine replaced Butzi Porsche, and at the top of the tree Dr Ernst Fuhrmann, who had been responsible for the original Carrera four-cam engine, became both managing and technical director. Almost as if in reaction to these changes, sales in 1972 picked up, to a total of 14,503 cars.

One of the first things to happen that must have pleased Ernst Fuhrmann was the reappearance of the name Carrera. This appelation had a special

Above: By the late 1970s the 911 came in two forms, the sleek, standard coupe (background) or the brutal Turbo (foreground) with those flared wheel arches and huge rear spoiler.

Left: Nothing to tell you this 911 cockpit is anything out of the ordinary, but in fact it belongs to a Carrera RS 2.7. Confusingly you could get the model minus all non-essentials or fully trimmed as here.

Right: Arguably one of the greatest all-round cars ever, and today ultra-desirable: the immortal Carrera 2.7 RS.

meaning in the Porsche dictionary, and the 911 Carrera was to be no exception – it would become one of the most sought-after Porsches ever.

The Carrera was first seen at Paris in October 1972. It was an homologation special, intended for Group 4 (Special GT) racing which required 500 manufactured. Selling 500 racers was *not* something the sales staff looked on with favor. Since it didn't conform to American regulations they couldn't sell it there. They crossed their fingers and hoped. They needn't have bothered – a week after the show they had sold their 500, by April 1973 the 1000th had been produced and homologated for Production GT (Group 3) by July that year, and at the end of the model year about 1600 had been built.

What did a Carrera buyer get for his money? First of all, yet another increase in capacity, to 2687cc (which meant the car could also be entered in up to 3-liter classes) bringing the power output up to 210bhp at 6300rpm. Then there were seven-inch wide wheels at the back, covered by wide, flared arches, and six-inchers at the front. The interior was detrimmed. Heavier anti-roll bars and Bilstein gas-filled dampers were fitted all round.

And it looked *so* right. There was a deep dam under the nose, but even more astonishing was a strange growth on the rear lid – it looked like, and was promptly named, a 'duck-tail.' This served four purposes: it reduced lift quite considerably; it improved the drag coefficient; it moved the center of air pressure back, which helped straight line stability in cross winds and high speed corners; and it helped cooling since the high pressure area was above the cooling vents. It also helped to keep the tail lights clean!

You could have a Carrera in any color so long as it was white, but there was a choice of colors, either red, green or blue, for the amazing 'Carrera' logo along the side, another of Tony Lapine's efforts.

It looked stunning, and had the performance to match. It had a top speed around the 150mph mark, reached 60mph from a standstill in 5½ seconds, and generated 0.9g lateral acceleration when cornering.

The 1974 model year saw a contraction in the 911 range. All models received the 2.7-liter engine, but in different states of tune and output.

In addition to the bigger engine, the 1973/74 models, the G series, received Bosch's K-Jetronic fuel injection system, except for the Carrera which retained the mechanical layout.

The most distinctive alteration, however, was the appearance of heavier bumpers front and rear, to meet the American regulations which required them to be assaulted by a massive pendulum. Porsche perhaps expected an outcry similar to that which created the bigger bumpers on the 356B. In fact Tony Lapine and his team managed to integrate the design very successfully indeed, so much so that it made the earlier ones look positively dainty.

October 1974 saw yet another Porsche landmark, the introduction of the immortal 911 Turbo, but let us for the moment bring the story of the unblown cars up to date. In 1975 the Turbo's 3-liter die-cast aluminum block appeared in the Carrera 3. With this increase in capacity, peak power increased slightly to 230bhp, and flexibility improved to give a more tractable machine for traffic driving. Thus the Carrera 3 replaced the 911S, so simplifying the range to the Turbo, the Carrera 3 and the 2.7-liter 911. The latter virtually took over from the 911S, with an output (165bhp) roughly between that of the earlier 911 (150bhp) and the S (175bhp). With the introduction of the I and J series models in August 1975, all the 911 bodies were fully rust-proofed via the use of Thyssen galvanized steel for all panels.

1974 and 1975 were bad years for Porsche, following the Yom Kippur war and the fuel shortage, with production falling to 11,624 and 9710 respectively, so it was not too surprising when changes over the next couple of years were kept to a minimum. Thus it wasn't until the usual mid-year announcements in 1977 that the next major changes were made to the model range. The most important was the simplification, yet again, of the range: the Carrera 3 and 911 were replaced by the 3-liter 911SC. This model retained the Turbo luxury features such as the automatic heating control, and the Carrera 3's flared arches, but with the 911S's pressure-cast alloy wheels that first appeared in 1974. The engine was a slightly detuned Carrera unit giving 180bhp but again with more flexibility and little loss of performance. A Sport model, with front and rear spoilers, 16-inch wheels with 185 and 205/50 tires, and uprated shock absorbers appeared too. In 1980 a rise in compression ration, to 9.8:1, gave an increase in power, to 204bhp.

More than once in its lifetime the 911 has been killed off by the pundits – and it was very nearly killed off by Professor Fuhrmann in the late 1970s. He saw the future of the company lying with the 924/944 and 928 series, and in this he clashed with Ferry Porsche. In the end, there was a parting of the

Above: Pure muscle – the Porsche 911 Turbo (or Type 930 following Porsche nomenclature), one of the acknowledged great Supercars. That vast rear spoiler is rubber-edged for safety reasons.

Left: Three generations of the charismatic Carrera – a 1964 356, a 1972 RS 2.7 and a 1986 3.0.

Above right: Cockpit of a 1984 Cabriolet, with later instruments, steering wheel and plenty of leather.

Right: Porsche revive a famous name – with its cut-down windshield and humpy tonneau cover, the 1989 Speedster is a 1980s re-creation of the 1950s 356 Speedster.

ways, and Fuhrmann was replaced by a German-born American engineer, Peter Schutz, on 1 January 1981.

Among his other briefs he was given the job of revitalizing the 911 models. A clue to the future was given at the 1981 Frankfurt Show, in the form of a 'Studie' which consisted of a 911 Turbo with a fully convertible body and four-wheel drive.

The completely open shell was not a difficult modification to make to the base Targa, and the only real wonder was that it had taken Porsche so long. In fact, rumor has it that one was running around Weissach before Schutz's appearance on the scene – but not when Fuhrmann was about . . . Thus it was no surprise when the 911SC Cabriolet, to give it an official title, was unveiled at the Geneva Show in March 1982. The soft top stowed neatly when down, looked smooth when raised, and featured a zip-out rear window. Initially it was manually operated, but later power assistance was added. The new model immediately proved popular, and in its first year of production outsold the Targa by 4277 to 2752.

Later that year the Carrera name was resurrected once more, for the unblown models, and to go with it was an increase in capacity to 3164cc, via the 74.4mm stroke from the Turbo. Naturally this led to an increase in power

– 231bhp at 5900rpm – and torque, but with no fuel consumption penalty thanks to the introduction of Bosch's DME engine management system. A distinctive feature of these Carreras was the use of 'telephone dial' wheels à la 928, with the traditional fivespoke items as an optional extra.

Another optional extra, though a highly expensive one, was the M-491 Sport Equipment body kit which converts the standard Coupe, Targa or Cabrio into a Turbo look-alike with wide, flared rear wheel arches and huge rear spoiler.

The annual model changes continued, though in minor form – a revised facia in 1985, a new gear-change pattern in 1986, for example – until the Frankfurt Motor Show, as ever, in 1987. On display was yet *another* variant of the 911.

From the waist down it looked like a Cabrio, but the standard windshield had been severely chopped and lowered, and a rigid, humpy tonneau covered the soft top in its well behind the seats. It looked startling enough in that guise, but in fact the windshield could be removed altogether, and a full rigid plastic tonneau covering the whole cockpit, with but a small slot-like opening for the driver's head, could be added. In this form it looked uncannily like an up-dated version of the fifties 356 Speedster, and that in fact is what it is: it's even called the Speedster. Those who remember the original ugly duckling love it: youngsters, unaware of Porsche's Speedster tradition, seem to regard it as hideous. Porsche themselves regard it very much as a Speedster for the late 1990s, and there may well be a one-make series of races for this model, similar in vein to the 944 Turbo Cup, when it goes into production in early 1989.

Somewhat over-shadowed by the Speedster was an equally intriguing version of the 911. It looked like a standard Carrera with the Sport Equipment option and the addition of a discreet 'CS' logo on the side. Inside it was very spartan compared to the standard model – there were no rear seats and not much sound damping, for example – and the ignition had been modified to allow the engine to rev to near enough 7000rpm, and to give 231bhp. A lightweight, more powerful Carrera? Sound familiar? Of course – the original 1973 Carrera 2.7. And that, indeed, is what the CS is, a 1990s version of the 2.7, a sports car that can be driven with equal ease on road or track. The initials stand for Club Sport, and it is aimed directly at the enthusiast who wants to race at club level and not in the major league, driving to and from events with the minimum of preparation. With its stiffened suspension, less weight and more power it naturally makes an ideal road car for the more enthusiastic driver too. There are those who predict that, like the 2.7, the Carrera CS is a classic of the future.

1988 saw the 911 celebrate its quarter century, and, late in the year, the world's press gathered down in Southern France to see and drive the latest model. What they saw and drove was, without doubt, the most radical 911 ever built.

The Carrera 4 was, in effect, a brand-new car. It *looked* like a 911, but that was about as far as it went: in all, 85 percent of components were new, and the 15 percent that weren't were confined mainly to the external panels.

The single most important factor in the Carrera 4 (given the in-house project number 964) was the four-wheel-drive system, developed from that of the 959. The center differential (which splits torque 30 percent front, 70 percent rear), is a planetary gear set with a multi-disk clutch, and is controlled by electronics which sense slip at each wheel and prevent it. The mechanical lay-out is almost a mirror-image of that adopted by Audi, with a central propellor shaft taking the drive from the gear-box to the front differential. The ancestry of the system can be traced back to 1955, and an aborted Jeep-type device, the Hunter, which was devised for the German army but never saw production.

The move to 4WD had meant a total redesign of the under-pinnings of the car with a new floor-pan, a larger transmission tunnel and reshaped luggage space up front. In addition there is full under-body panelling, giving a totally smooth passage to the air underneath: add a new, cleaner nose and tail and the drag factor drops from 0.395 to 0.32.

What becomes obvious on the move, and what will undoubtedly cause some amusement, is the retractable rear spoiler. At rest, it sits flush with the body, giving the classically clean 911 profile. However, at 50mph it is raised and extended by electric motors, only sitting down again when speed drops to a mere 6mph.

The suspension is all-new too. Up front, torsion bars have given way to coil springs, although MacPherson struts still look after the geometry. For the first time on a 911 there's power steering. At the back, too, there are coils instead of torsion bars, and though semi-trailing arms are retained for location there's an additional arm each side to give 'Weissach' geometry. Tire sizes are 205/55 at the front and 255/50 at the back. Naturally ABS is standard, and indeed some of the components are used for the 4WD control.

Finally, the engine. Though still an air-cooled flat six, it has come in for extensive revision. For a start the capacity has jumped to 3.6 liters, and there is dual ignition, developed from aircraft-engine experience. The outputs are 250bhp at 6100rpm, and 230lb/ft of torque at 4800rpm. For better sound damping, the engine has been partially encapsulated and, like all Porsches for the 1990s, it develops the same power outputs for all the world markets.

The Carrera 4 is more than just a new variant: it is indeed the basis for the 911 for the *next* quarter century. And, in that, the back-bone of the company.

Before we leave the unblown 911s, there is one variant that ought to be mentioned: the 912. With the demise of the 356 in March 1965, and the up-market move of the 911, there was a need for a model to plug the gap until the 911 was established. Porsche took the 911 body and running gear, but slotted in the 356's 1600cc flat four with either a four-speed or optional five-speed transmission, to create the 912.

It was, if anything, more successful than the 911! In its first year 6440 were made against 4865 of the 911, followed by 8700 the following year. In fact when production ceased in 1969 some 30,300 912s had been made. It was replaced by the 914/6 as the bottom rung Porsche.

But the 912 story wasn't finished. It was reintroduced for one year only, in 1975 (for the 1976 model year). It was sold only in America, at the insistence of Porsche + Audi, to act as a stop gap until the 924 arrived. The engine this time was a Porsche-developed 1971cc VW flat four, as seen in the last of the 914/4s, and produced 90bhp at 4900rpm. 2099 of these historic oddities were constructed.

But let us go from one extreme to the other, back to the year 1974. Porsche chose the Paris Salon to unveil one of the most charismatic cars they have ever made, and one which every Porscheophile who regards him-

Previous pages: By 1978, as on this SC, the 911's rear wheelarches had been extended sideways quite considerably but without damaging that lovely basic shape.

Above left: Subtlety is the name of the game — it may not look all that different, but beneath the skin the 911 Carrera 4 is a totally different animal with its 3.6-liter engine and four-wheel-drive.

Below left: For the Carrera 4, Porsche have kept the familiar face for 911 fanatics via a recognizable interior.

Top: When stationary, or at low speeds, the Carrera 4's rear spoiler sits flush with the engine cover.

Above: At speeds over 50mph the rear spoiler rises into position automatically.

Right: Ferdinand Alexander ('Butzi') Porsche with a model of the 911 Targa, one of his most famous creations.

self as a true enthusiast considers the ultimate road car – the 911 Turbo. It was Porsche's project number 930, and is often called that, but it is still officially the 911 Turbo. As with Carrera, it was intended to be an homologation special to meet impending new regulations for 1976.

Visually, with its deep front spoiler, large 'tea-tray' rear wing, hunky wheel arches enclosing Pirelli CN36 tires of 185 section at the front and 215 at the rear, the Turbo most resembled the racing Carrera RSR. From that car too came the aluminum block and cylinder dimensions, and thus the capacity of 2994cc. However the compression ratio was dropped to 6.5:1, but the increase in capacity, from the Carrera RS's 3 liters, helped recover some of the power lost when the engine was running at low speed and small throttle openings, before the turbocharger came 'on song.'

The turbocharger was by KKK, and K-Jetronic fuel injection was installed. To reduce the fabled turbo lag to a minimum, there was a by-pass in the inlet manifold, to keep compressor revs up to their working speed of the order of 90,000 to 100,000rpm. With the compressor free-wheeling, as it were, only minimal exhaust gases are needed to retain rotational speeds. To limit ultimate boost, a wastegate was fitted on the exhaust side. In this form the engine produced a splendid 260bhp.

Although the 911 had been steadily developed to take the increasing power outputs from, first, the 2.4- and then the 2.7-liter engines, 260bhp obviously required even more up-rating. A stronger, four-speed transmission had been designed and installed. The big fat wheels demanded reworked suspension, which included stronger bearings and altered settings. One byproduct was that the rear sheet metalwork had to be strengthened, and because of this a Targa version of the Turbo was not as first offered by the factory.

One major difference between the homologation special Carrera RS and the Turbo was that the former was a stripped machine with luxury touches as optional for road-going cars, but Fuhrmann insisted that the Turbo be as fully equipped as possible, almost to the 'cost no object' stage. It would be the flagship of the Porsche range.

Like the Carrera RS again, Porsche under-anticipated the demand that this sensational new car would create. In the 1975 model year, remembering it was only seen in public for the first time in October 1974, 274 Turbos were made. In the 1976 model year, this increased to 1184 road cars and 30 racers. The Turbo would never reach the figures of the lesser breeds, or even the 928, but it was a viable seller.

As ever, Porsche's mid-year press announcements in 1977 had something interesting to say. Apart from the introduction of the SC to replace the Carrera and the 911, the Turbo was uprated yet again. The bore and stroke were both increased to give a capacity of 3299cc, an intercooler was fitted, and the result was a nice, even power output of 300bhp. By this time, too, the Turbo had been sitting on Pirelli's P7s, giving tire widths of 205 section at the front and 225 at the back. In this 300bhp form the Turbo soldiered on for nearly a decade with very few changes. (Fuhrmann's policy of running down the 911 was never more apparent than with the Turbo.) In 1982 the exhaust system was modified to give less back pressure and the ignition timing optimized: power stayed constant, but torque rose from 303 to 318 lb/ft. 1984 saw central locking and electrically-adjustable seats plus larger diameter anti-roll bars, and 1985 saw wider rear wheels to take 245/45V16 tires. Tinkering, maybe – but the Turbo was still one of the great Supercars, and *Autocar* recorded a maximum speed of 162mph, with 60mph from a standstill appearing in a mere 5.1 seconds.

However, Schutz had turned his eye onto the Turbo by then, and asked the question that many Porsche fanatics had been asking for a long time: why no Targa or Cabrio versions of the Turbo? The traditional answer was always that the Turbo was too powerful for these shells. The lie to this was given by the innumerable German specialists who blithely converted Coupes into open cars with no apparent ill effects. The engineers, with Schutz pushing them, eventually gave in, and in 1987 the official Turbo Cabrio and Targa appeared on the scene, with suitable strengthening around the floorpan.

Those specialists gave Porsche another headache. Not only did they chop the roofs off Coupes, they 'customized' some by converting the nose to 935 form, with the tops of the wings and headlamps removed, giving a plain, flat, sloping front. Then, in 1983, Mansour Ojjeh, the head of TAG who was paying for the FI engine, asked Porsche to build him a very special special, in effect a road-going 935. There was a 380bhp engine, a massive rear spoiler, extended rear fenders with air intakes on their leading edges – and a flat, sloping nose like the 935. Complete with walnut dash and leather upholstery, the car was said to be capable of over 190mph.

In fact, Porsche's Customer Department had been able to offer the 'Flachbau' (flat nose) for quite some time, but mainly to racing teams. However, the advent of the Ojjeh car, plus the efforts of such as Rinspeed, Koening, b+b, *et al*, led Porsche to offer in-house conversions under Rolf Sprenger's Service and Customer Liaison Department. There was soon a semi-production line for Flachbau models and Sprenger and his men were turning out one a day. That still wasn't enough, though, and in 1988 the Flachbau models were incorporated into the production line in the new Works 5 building. The conversion is viciously expensive: in England, for example, at the time of writing, the standard Turbo Cabrio costs £63,300 ($110,775), while the Flachbau model (or, as it is cumbersomely called, the 911 Turbo with Sport

Above left: The ultimate road-going production Porsche 911 to date. The Turbo with Sport Equipment body kit, which includes the 'Flachbau' flat nose, derived from the racing 935.

Far left and left: The 1973 version of the car above, the Carrera 2.7 RS, with its exceedingly rare and desirable successor, the 1974 RSR.

Right: With its fat tires and Turbo-like rear spoiler, even the standard 911 of 1989 looks aggressive.

Equipment) costs nearly double – £109,100 ($190,925)! Mind you, you also get more power – 330bhp – thanks to a larger turbocharger and intercooler, modified camshafts and exhaust system, which gives a maximum speed of 171mph and 0-62mph takes a mere 5.2 seconds. *That*, as they say, is very quick indeed.

To drive a 911 Turbo is the experience of a lifetime. It can be mildly disappointing at first. You expect low speed temperament, poor town manners, a raucous engine – after all, isn't that what driving supercars is all about? Yet the Turbo is as docile as any family saloon (though you have to keep reminding yourself that it's wider than it looks from inside). And *that* is what separates the Turbo from other supercars. It is totally practical, yet its acceleration, roadholding, handling, braking and effortless speed are superior to almost everything else on the road.

But, of course, the 911 Turbo Flachbau is not the ultimate 911. That honor must go to a model that has so little in common with the basic 911 that it is known by its type number 959. In fact, to call it a 911 is a little like saying that New York is simply the original town of York in England, with additions.

The 959 came about, like the 917 racer, because of a rule change in motor sport which created Group B. This called for a minimum build of 200 cars but with a wide-open specification. (Group A is for production cars with a minimum 5000 off, Group C is for sports-racers, in which Porsche, with the 956 and 962, are dominant). Quite apart from racing in Group B, the 959 was intended to enter and rule the world of rallying at a time when the Audi quattro with its four-wheel-drive was annihilating everything in sight. When the 959 first appeared, as a 'Gruppe B Studie' at Frankfurt in 1983, it looked as if it would carry off its aims with ease.

The only part common between the 959 and the 911 is the basic galvanized steel monocoque skeleton, though the engine is still a flat six in the tail. From there on in, it's all new.

The bodywork from window level down is made from Kevlar, except for the doors and front luggage lid which are aluminum. The headlamp shape is a cross between standard and Flachbau, and all the better for it. The fenders are widely flared front and rear (the 959 is 10in wider than a 911), with assorted intakes for cooling air. At the rear there's a beautifully formed spoiler which wraps up and over the engine cover. The whole is superbly integrated, smooth and clean, and this is born out by the drag factor of 0.32 with, perhaps more importantly, zero lift at 200mph.

The engine is derived from that of the 956/962 racers. The capacity is 2857cc, and there are four-valve, water-cooled heads (which coincidentally help enormously when it comes to cockpit heating!). There are twin KKK turbochargers, but designed to run in sequence, so that at low revs only one works. But above 4000rpm the other cuts in, to minimize lag yet give high boost – 2bar, or 28psi – at high revs. Electronics control waste-gate pressure. Uniquely, the engine will run on unleaded fuel and, if required, a catalyst can be added. The power output is 450bhp at 6500rpm, and torque 369lb/ft at 5500rpm, which makes it arguably the most powerful engine ever offered in a road car by any manufacturer.

And that power is taken to all four wheels via a six-speed gearbox and a unique 4WD system. The mechanical layout of the standard 911 lends itself easily to 4WD since a propeller shaft can be run directly from the gearbox to the front wheels without any side-steps to avoid the engine as is necessary with front-engined 4WD cars. Between the gearbox and the front differential there's a multi-plate clutch which acts as a differential: torque transmission depends on how tightly the clutch disks are clamped together. This operation is controlled electronically so that when sensors at each wheel detect slip the electronics either apply or reduce pressure on the clutch plates and direct torque to the wheel with most grip.

The suspension is pure racing, with wishbones and coils at each corner,

Left: Dreams for sale – only 200 examples of the incredible, and incredibly complex, 959 were made, and each became an instant investment. Porsche made a loss on every one.

Right: The interior of the 959 is instantly recognizable as 911-derived.

Below: The rear spoiler wraps up and over the engine cover.

Bottom: The 959 power house, putting out 450bhp at 6500rpm. The 959 is not for mere mortals.

but with dual shock absorbers, one of which is electronically controlled. These react to both speed and cornering forces, keeping ride height constant (and adjustable) and acting as an anti-roll bar. There's power steering, and the massive tires, 235/45s at the front and 255/40s at the rear, are fitted with pressure sensing in each to detect any deflation. A puncture at 200mph could be a mite fraught! The brakes are from the 962 as well, and naturally ABS is standard.

The 959 is, without doubt, the most complex, expensive, and quickest car on the road today, and an example of the highest technology at which Porsche excel. Alas, its competition potential never really materialized. It was a long time in the development stage, partly because of Porsche's insistence that the road cars be true and luxurious road cars, not just thinly disguised racers, partly because of supplier delay. But most of the delay was because no-one took up Group B racing and then, midway through 1986, the FIA cancelled Group B in rallying because speeds were becoming simply silly. However, the 959 *did* score one notable success, in the infamous Paris-Daker Raid in 1986. I was lucky enough to visit the factory in late 1987, and watch 959s being assembled. Apparently the first ones took 3500 man-hours to make, but by then this had been reduced to 1500. When the 959 was first announced in 1984 the price was set at a massive DM420,000. In the end, though, this figure must have seemed a bargain, for it actually cost considerably more than that to make (how much more Porsche won't say!), and with those man-hour figures it's easy to see why. The lucky buyers of 959s found they could sell them for double or more what they paid for them.

I was also lucky enough to be driven round the test track at Weissach in a production 959 by one of the test drivers, Gunther Steckonig. To quote from the story I wrote in *Autosport* at the time:

'He hits the start point, and floors the throttle. The sheer acceleration is stunning, like nothing I've ever felt before in a road car. Into a fast, dropping, sweeping, banked left-hander, and – just for a moment – it feels as if I'm going to black out! Over a blind right-hander, the car feeling utterly stable, but you notice that there appears to be a lot of understeer – he's winding on a fair bit of lock. The main straight: again there's that sense of awesome acceleration, the engine taking on a hard bark. The last corner, and he's off full throttle onto full braking – it's like being accelerated backwards. Into the corner at what seems an impossible speed: the 959 simply squats down and around.

We've covered 2.5kms in a matter of seconds. There has not been nearly enough time to carry out any sort of evaluation – it's a total sensory overload situation, like being being caught up in a whirlpool for a few seconds, leaving you dazed and bewildered. Dear God, the 959 is not for mere mortals . . .'

The Alternative Porsche

Previous pages: The people's Porsche – more or less – in the form of the 914/6.

Above: Apart from wheels and badging, the 914/6 was indistinguishable from the 914/4. Both featured a mid-mounted engine, but that in the 4 was a VW unit, that in the 6 a Porsche.

Left: One of the few Porsches that wasn't shaped in-house, the 914 didn't bear any family resemblance to the 911s.

Above right: A VW-powered 914/4. All 914s were Targa-topped.

In the late 1950s and early 1960s the mid-engined configuration had ousted the conventional layout in the highest form of motor racing, Formula 1. The standards set there began to trickle down to production cars, slowly but surely. The world's press predicted that most sportscars would be made that way before long. The advantages were obvious from the track: better road-holding and handling. The disadvantages didn't become apparent until mid-engined cars actually appeared on the scene: awkward engine accessibility, a noise source close to the cockpit, poor luggage space, and in many instances, poor visibility.

But in 1966 mid-engined sportscars were all the rage. Naturally Porsche, with their racing experience, could build such a car. The loss of the 356 meant a lack of cheap Porsches: something mid-engined could replace it. Go back to first principles — use VW parts.

VW too could do with an image booster. The Beetle continued as ever, but potential replacements such as the Type 2 just hadn't caught on in the same way. There'd been the Karmann-Ghia, a plain jane in a party frock, but it didn't have a sporty image.

The solution to both problems seemed logical: a VW-Porsche. Using the mass-production abilities of the Wolfsburg company and Zuffenhausen brains, the result could be a car of considerable sales potential. It could even be made in two versions: a downmarket Porsche and an upmarket VW. One can see the appeal of the idea. Nordhoff and Ferry came to a formal agreement that Porsche would design a new sports car for VW — and an informal one that Porsche could use the model as a basis for a cheap Porsche as well.

The first problem to crop up was the look of the car. To satisfy both companies, an outside consultant company, Gugelot Design, a well-known industrial design firm, were employed. They had styled a car for the chemical company Bayer, who were trying to promote a new structural material, using BMW mechanicals. It was this car that caught VW and Porsche's eyes, and Gugelot were given the job. The bodyshell was a monocoque structure, with bulkheads in front of and behind the front-mounted gas tank, between cockpit and engine, and aft of the engine, in front of the rear trunk. With two trunks, one in the nose and the other in the tail, luggage space was commendable. The cockpit too was roomy — but only for two people.

The front suspension and steering was pure 911. At the rear semi-trailing arms located the wheels which were suspended on coil springs with integral shock absorbers.

There were two power units. For the VW car there was new flat-four engine fitted to the VW 411. With a capacity of 1679cc, and Bosch electronic fuel injection, it produced 80bhp at 4900rpm. The version of the 914 so equipped was called the 914/4.

The other engine was Porsche's own flat-six, kept in a 2-liter form for this application after it had been enlarged to 2.2 liters for the 911.

And then tragedy struck. In July 1967 Heinz Nordhoff fell ill, and died in April 1968. His successor, Kurt Lotz, had only joined VW a few months before. He wasn't aware of the working relationship between Ferry Porsche and Nordhoff, particularly the verbal agreement in which Porsche could use 914 components for the 914/6. Lotz looked at the agreement which simply

said that Porsche had designed a car for VW, who had complete rights to it. If Porsche wanted trimmed bodyshells from Karmann, he would have to pay the going rate – which was actually more than that for the 911. So much for a cheap Porsche.

To market the car, a new company was set up in Germany, owned 50/50 by VW and Porsche. In America Lotz wanted to sell the up-market Audi, but wondered if the VW image would drag it down. In America Porsche would give up its autonomy and combine with VW to form Porsche + Audi. The 914 would be known as the VW-Porsche, except in America where it would be a straight-forward Porsche.

At its launch in 1969 at Frankfurt, the 914/4 and 914/6 received a mixed reception. When the press got their hands on the cars, they tended to prefer the extra performance of the 914/6, not unnaturally, and in general the car's handling was judged as above average to good. But so was the basic 911's.

That the 914/6 was a Porsche can never be doubted – it followed truly in the path of Ferry's original 356. The trouble was that there were those two letters, V and W, associated with it. Even in America, where it was pure Porsche, enthusiasts of the marque didn't take to it. Not just because of the VW connection, but because of the looks as well. Those who judged cars purely on merit found it a good car with excellent roadholding and handling, except at the ultimate limit.

By 1970 it was becoming obvious that the 914/6 just had the wrong image, cost too much, and wasn't accepted as a Porsche. An attempt to inject some life into it came in 1971, when some pre-production cars were made with 2.4-liter Porsche engines, flared wheel arches covering fat 185/79 x 15 Michelin tires, color-keyed front bumper-cum spoiler and rear bumper, and a rooftop welded in place. They were named the 916. Two weeks before they were due to go on show at Paris the project was cancelled. A total of 3360 914/6s were made, sales towards the end in 1972 becoming a mere trickle.

The 914/4 continued for much longer and was much more successful, though, through to 1975 by which time it had been gradually improved and given more performance to go with its handling, first with a 1.8-liter and final-

ly a 2-liter VW engine. At the end of its life the 914/4 was a much better and more reliable car, and in total 115,646 were produced.

The 914/6 project was killed by four things. The unworkability of the combined German VW-Porsche marketing company and internal politics. The second reason was cost. Thirdly it was regarded as too ugly. And finally, the car that should have been all things to all men finished up being not much to anyone – until it went out of production, and promptly became a cult car, like the 356 Speedster – except that there were fewer 914/6's than Speedsters.

Left: The nearly car. The 916, a 914/6 with 2.4-liter engine, fixed roof, wide wheels and color-keyed bumpers very nearly saw production but was cancelled at the last minute.

Below left: The 914's pop-up headlamps did nothing for looks or aerodynamics.

Right: A few attempts to restyle the 914 were made by outsiders – this is Ital Design's Tapiro, dating from 1970.

Below: The 916 had the potential to be a Ferrari Dino beater, in performance if not in looks.

Role Reversal

I can well remember the launch of the 924. Everyone present had but one thought as the Germans, with Teutonic thoroughness, went through every little detail of the car – was it a 'real' Porsche? How would died-in-the-wool Porscheophiles react to it?

For the car was as complete a break from tradition as any manufacturer has ever made. It wasn't rear engined, it wasn't air cooled. It's Audi/VW parentage wasn't hidden. Previous attempts at 'cheap' Porsches hadn't been all that successful, yet here was a car on which Porsche were going to, had no option but to, stake their future.

Only later did the realization come that in fact Porsche were following one of their longest traditions of all. What else had the first 356 coupe been but a lightweight machine based on VW mechanicals?

Yet there was another reason for its more humble componentry: as always, Porsche's external design and development section had been working hard and with considerable financial reward, and one of their contracts had been VW project 425, initiated by Rudolf Leiding, the man who converted VW from Beetle to Rabbit, from 1930's thinking to 1980's. He liked the idea of a 2+2 coupe, a sporty machine, more so than Audi's own 100 coupe. Project 425 was the result. However Leiding was replaced by Tony Schmücker who killed the project. Porsche took a gamble and a decision – *they* would make the car. Part of the deal involved in buying back the project would be that VW/Audi would build the car in the ex-NSU Neckarsulm factory. This killed three birds with one stone: it meant that VW/Audi didn't have to close down a redundant factory and thus find a way of sacking the workforce; it gave Porsche much needed additional production capacity; and it was quite close to Zuffenhausen and thus in Swabia, an area of traditional hard work and craftsmanship which Porsche valued highly, and close enough for Porsche to keep tabs on quality and other facets of production.

From the beginning of the project, one factor was constant: the power unit. This was to be an overhead camshaft version of the then-current Audi 100, which was destined for VW's LT van, the post-1977 Audi 100s, and eventually the AMC Gremlin.

In the Audi it was connected directly to the transaxle, for the 100 was a front wheel drive car. Unlike the smaller Rabbits, Polos, and Sciroccos which used a transverse layout, the big Audi used an in-line arrangement, with the engine ahead of the axle center line and the transmission behind. With this as the basic building block, what were the options open to the engineers?

The obvious one was front wheel drive. Then there was rear engined, rear wheel drive, with the power train arranged *à la* 914. Or rear wheel drive again, but with engine and transaxle reversed, *à la* 911. Finally there was the 'old fashioned' front engine, rear wheel drive configuration.

The first choice was out since, right from the beginning Porsche, if not necessarily VW, foresaw much more powerful versions, and the conflicts of power and front wheel drive were considered too complex. The second was ruled out on the grounds that one of the big complaints regarding the 914 was that 'there wasn't room to store a raincoat' in the passenger compartment – mid-placed engines may be fine for handling and image, but tend to be impractical. In addition, the 928 was already on the drawing boards, and a large and relatively cumbersome V8 twixt people and driven wheels was even less practical, and the 924 and 928 were to be the Porsches of the future: there had to be a strong family connection between the two. The same reason meant that the 911 layout was unviable.

The layout chosen brought a number of additional advantages. Water cooling helped noise reduction, but so did separating the two major noise sources, engine and exhaust outlet. An engine at the front helped in overcoming crash protection regulations. Possibly most important of all, was that an equitable weight balance between front and rear could be attained, with consequent roadholding and handling advantages. It was strange indeed at that press launch to hear the engineers talking about the benefits of even balance when they had practically perfected the road manners of the 911 with its pretty massive rearward weight bias.

So: the engine had to go in the front. Where to put the transmission though? Directly behind the engine as in normal practice would have meant a new box since the Audi box-cum-differential didn't lay itself open to such modification, though the planned system for the VW LT van, which did have a conventional drive, was a possibility.

The answer was technically elegant and ingenious. The Audi engine/ transaxle was split behind the clutch, the transaxle moved aft and the engine left where it was. The two units were joined by a large diameter, backbone tube in which ran a small diameter propeller shaft. There were precedents

Previous pages: The 1989 Porsche 944, the latest in a line of models that stretches back to 1975.

Below left: The mid-1970s was a time of bright, day-glo colors, as this early 924 shows.

Right: This 1986 924 is recognizably a close descendent of the original 924 (seen *below* on its launch in the South of France) with differences which include a slim rubbing strip down the side, and a discreet rear spoiler.

for this set up, and Alfa Romeo adopted it too. And one can't help reflecting that, somewhere ingrained in Porsche thinking, was that *some* of the mechanicals had to go at the back . . .

The 1984cc engine, fitted with a Heron head (the bottom of the head is flat, the combustion chamber being formed in the piston) and Bosch K-Jetronic fuel injection, gave 125bhp in European form and 95bhp in detoxed, USA form. To say that most of the VW/Audi parts used in the suspension, steering and brakes, were straight from the parts bin is a gross over-simplification: Porsche added their own touches to ensure they came up to Porsche standards.

Clothing all these mechanical units was a distinctive new bodyshell. My own first reaction at that launch was that Tony Lapine's shape was curiously anonymous, almost bland, yet had a Porsche family feel to it. The nose, for example, with no obvious air intake, hearkened back to the rear-engined days. It was also rounded, smoothed, with large diameter curvature at a time when Giugiaro's trend-setting square edges – what Bill Mitchell of GM fame called 'the folded paper school of design' – was all the rage. It was not perhaps as timeless as the 911 which had and has weathered the years extremely well, but it wasn't going to date quickly either, and – for the technically minded – it had a (for then) excellent drag coefficient of 0.36. It was going to be an easy car to push through the air, with consequent benefits to speed in the upper ranges and fuel consumption.

I was probably still 911 orientated when I helped carry out one of the first full road tests of a 924 in Britain. Gone was that indescribable crackly beat from the tail, the sheer excitement of sling-shotting out of a curve, the exhilaration of a 911. In its place was a comfortable, spacious GT but not a car that got the adrenalin flowing from the moment you switched on the key. The engine sounded fussy and harsh at high revs, wind and road noise (especially over bumps) were obtrusive, and the gearshift, not perhaps surprisingly considering that the synchromesh had to deal with the inertia of the propeller shaft as well, graunched on snatched changes. And inside there was more than a whiff of VW cost-cutting about it. Perhaps because it was a Porsche I expected too much.

It's positive points really only emerged after spending more time with one. It was deceptive in many ways. The performance, for example. In a 911, almost every cross-country trip was a semi-race. In the 924 you would cover the ground nearly as quickly but with very little drama. The roadholding was excellent, and the handling superb, being to all intents and purposes neutral

and vice free. And there were a lot of more mundane factors going for it – such as the comparatively vast luggage space, easy to get at via a huge lift-up rear window instead of fighting it past seats. The excellent fuel consumption. The steering that was oh-so-correct. It wasn't a 911: it *was* a Porsche but of a new breed. And time will tell whether the zinc-coated sheet metal from which the 924 is made, and which allows Porsche to offer a 7 year anti-corrosion guarantee, really does work.

As ever, the base 924 has been gradually modified over its lifetime. Barely little more than a year after the first production cars rolled off the new Neckarsulm assembly line, in late 1975, the first important change was made: the VW/Audi three-speed automatic transmission became available, while American market cars became more powerful.

Late 1977 saw another important change; a five-speed Porsche-designed transmission was offered as an optional extra. This particular box would last but a short time: in 1979 for the 1980 model season it would be replaced as standard with one in which fifth was out on a limb, unlike the 1977 box in which first was the odd one out. Fully transistorized ignition, a smaller steering wheel and 'black chrome' trim were also offered at the same time.

1979 saw major development number one for the 924, however: the addition of a turbocharger to create the 924 Turbo. In true Porsche tradition this was no bolt-on goodie but a thorough engineering job, enough to make the Turbo a new model.

Externally the 924 Turbo was instantly recognizable from the front by the row of four air vents across the nose of the hood to increase cooling air flow and a duct to one side of the hood. At the rear there was a discreet polyurethane spoiler around the bottom of the window.

Driving the 924 Turbo showed how much Porsche had improved matters over even a brief period. Not only was the Turbo a considerably quicker machine, but it was even more deceptively so, as Porsche deemed a boost pressure gauge unnecessary – and it was difficult to tell when the blower was in operation or not, since there was no sudden surge or high pitched whistle to say that the turbocharger was doing its work. And work on refinement too had paid off: only wind noise was below par, though the ride wasn't helped by the fatter tires.

The 1979 Frankfurt Show saw a famous name applied to what was alleged to be a one-off show car. The name was Carrera, and it was basically a 924 Turbo with flared wheel arches and fat tires. In June 1980, however, Porsche made it official. They announced the Carrera GT as an homologation special

Above and below left: One of the more exciting 924s was the Turbo, easily distinguishable by the row of vents across the nose, a NACA duct on the hood, and two-tone paintwork.

Right: The addition of the turbocharger and its attendant pipework meant a very full engine bay.

Above: The last of the 924 line, the 1987-version with the 944 engine.

Left: The Porsche-manufactured slant four engine which replaced the Audi-made unit in the 924S.

Above right: A base 944 and its anything-but-base sister, a Carrera GT, with a production run limited to 400.

with a production run of 400 cars. As they said, 'It is intended to succeed the classic 1973 lightweight Carrera (the 911) as the ultimate road car with competition potential.'

The 924 became the quickest-selling Porsche ever, with the 100,000 mark coming up in five years – but it was a variable feast. When the Deutschemark/dollar ratio was favorable, sales in America soared: when it wasn't, they slumped. It tended to be regarded as an upmarket car for what it had to offer, and the most important item on offer was the name. Compared to its competitors from Japan, such as the Mazda RX7, which gave a similar (or at least sufficient) performance, plus higher levels of trim, it was expensive. Sales dropped in the States from a peak of 13,700 in 1977 to 5,400 in 1980, and in 1983 it was withdrawn from the American market.

Over the second five years of its life the 924 received scant attention. There was the limited edition Le Mans 924 in 1980, to commemorate its first appearance at the Sarthe circuit. It featured some Turbo items, such as the rear spoiler, plus 15in wheels with 60-series tires, stiffer dampers and thicker anti-roll bars, and a leather interior. Of the standard 924s, this model is arguably the most collectable. For 1982, the roof loading was uprated, for 1983 the rear spoiler was standardized, and so on, but this was really just playing around, because its days were numbered for a very simple reason. Audi had dropped the 2-liter, 4-cylinder engine from their range.

In 1985 the Audi unit was replaced by Porsche's own slant-four, and the model was renamed the 924S. Since the 924's body was slimmer than that of the 944, and was fitted with narrower wheels and tires, it therefore had less frontal area which could well make it quicker than its more expensive sister! Thus the engine as installed in the 924S was detuned slightly to 150bhp, but it also meant that it gave the same power with or without a catalyst. This was sufficient to propel the S to a maximum of 134mph, and to 60mph from a standstill in 8.0 sec as recorded by *Autocar*. But perhaps more importantly it moved the entry-level Porsche model away from its Audi image. That,

though, is not to decry the original: it sold over 130,000 in its lifetime, making it Porsche's best-seller ever. And you can't do better than that.

The 924S survived only for three years, being dropped from the range in 1988, when a change of Porsche policy (and directors) saw everything moved up a class or two. There was, simply, no room for a 'cheap' Porsche.

Le Mans 1981 saw one of the world's worst-kept secrets appear on the track. It was powered by a turbocharged four-cylinder engine right enough, but had a four-valve head and twin overhead camshafts, giving 410bhp and 180mph timed along the Mulsanne straight. But it was more than just a one-off prototype. It heralded the new, all-Porsche engine.

Porsche announced the 944, as the new model was called, at the Frankfurt Show in September 1981. It looked basically like the Carrera GT with its wide-hipped fenders and rear spoiler. The chassis and running gear were developed versions of those of the 924. It was what was under the bonnet that caused all the fuss.

It was a slant four, true, but its heritage came from Porsche, not VW/Audi. To say that it was half of the 928's V8 is a fairly massive generalization, but that is basically what it was. It had a capacity of 2479cc, quite large for an in-line four, and such engines tend to be rough. Porsche had heeded the grumbles about the harshness and vibration of the early 924s, and went out of their way to make the 944 engine smoother. They did this by adding twin balance shafts, one down near the crankshaft, the other up near the head, running at twice engine speed. Then there were very special engine mounts. This may sound complicated, but having tried a PRV (the cooperative Peugeot-Renault-Volvo) V6, and another V6 based on three quarters of the 928 V8, for a variety of reasons including smoothness and assembly difficulties, the straight four was chosen. The 163bhp this engine produces slots it neatly between the 125bhp of the standard 924 and the 177bhp of the Turbo.

The arrival of the 944 saw a more favorable Deutschemark/dollar rate, and soon the 944 became a hot seller: in the 1983 model year some 23,200

Left: One of the most significant variants of the 944 was the Turbo, giving 220bhp at 5800rpm.

Below left: The 944 Turbo's power plant which, boosted to 250bhp, formed the basis of a highly successful one-make race series in Europe.

Below: The Tony Lapine lines of the 944 are timeless, helped from 1985 on by its smoother front end.

Right: The 944S looked little different from the outside, but under the bonnet was a 16-valve engine.

were built, surpassing the 924's best year. Sales in the US were helped by the fact that, following Porsche's new principles, the power output was the same whether catalysts were fitted or not. And the more aggressive looks, with those wider, more svelte wheel arches, didn't hurt one little bit.

And there was performance to match: *Autocar* measured the top speed at 137mph, and the 0-60mph time at 7.4 sec. More significantly for the on-the-road performance, though, was a lovely, fat torque curve, which gave a minimum of 144lb/ft between 2500 and 5500rpm, while the peak was 151lb/ft at a mere 3000rpm. In other words, here was a car that didn't need the use of all the revs – no matter how smooth the engine, thanks to the balancer shafts – to go very quickly. It was a *relaxed* high-performance car.

And, naturally, there were variants. One of the obvious steps was to add a turbocharger, and early in 1985 the world's press was taken to Porsche's now-traditional launch pad, the Mas d'Artigny in southern France, to meet the new model.

For the Turbo, the base 944 was thoroughly reworked. The turbocharger was a state-of-the-art KKK unit, water cooled, and boost was controlled electronically via the engine management system. The output was an impressive 220bhp at 5800rpm, and torque a truck-like 243lb/ft at 3500rpm. The transmission, suspension and brakes were all up-rated to cope with the extra performance, while the bodywork was cleaned up. The nose incorporated a

new one-piece molding, similar to that of the 928, the windshield was flush mounted, there were aerodynamic plates fitted beneath the engine and the underbody, and at the rear there was a sub-bumper wing. The net result was not only a smoother looking car but a reduction in drag to a Cd of 0.33.

The 944 Turbo became the basis of a hugely successful race series in Germany in 1986. The cars ran with the standard 220bhp engines, but a roll cage was fitted, the suspension was lowered, Bilstein adjustable dampers were adopted, and trim could be removed to pare down weight. For 1987 competitors were allowed to raise the power to 250bhp, via a bigger turbocharger and higher boost settings, and a road-going, limited edition of 1000 was produced. These had a maximum speed of 161mph, and arrowed to 60mph in 5.5 sec, which put them firmly in 911 territory!

The second significant 944 variant was the 944S, announced in late 1986. The important feature of this model was a new, twin-cam, 16-valve head atop the slant-four engine. Most such engines are designed to give a much higher output, but that of the S was really needed to cope with ever-increasing emission controls without loss of performance for such markets as America and Japan. Indeed, when it was announced it gave the same power – 190bhp at 6000rpm – with or without a catalysor. Torque too improved to 181lb/ft, but it now peaked at 4300rpm. Thus, in terms of power and performance, the 944S slotted in between the standard 944 and the Turbo, but could be sold in the same form worldwide.

The third important 944 first appeared as one of the proverbial 'Studies' at Frankfurt in 1985: a drop-head. (It was also fitted with the 16-valve engine from the S, as a matter of interest.) Various specialists had produced their own version, but none matched the overall neatness of Porsche's in-house efforts. The 944 Cabriolet, though, was a long time a-coming, and it wasn't until March 1988 that the production version appeared, ready to go on sale later that year.

With the 944 range completed, Porsche looked set to enjoy successful years in 1987 and 1988 – and then near-disaster struck with the infamous Wall Street stock market crash in late 1987. Porsche were hard hit. Not, sur-

prisingly, in the 911/928 sector – the *very* rich could still afford expensive toys – but in the 4-cylinder segment. Sales of the 944 dropped off alarmingly, and at one point the factory was working a one week on, one off system. Schutz resigned by mutual agreement, replaced by Heinz Branitzki.

But the folks at Porsche are nothing if not fighters, and late in 1988 a totally revamped 944 line was introduced, while the 924S was dropped.

The base 944 8-valve engine was given an increase in capacity, from 2.5 to 2.7 liters via a 4mm bigger bore. A higher compression ratio, bigger inlet valves, retuned electronics and altered valve timing combined with the increase in capacity gave a slight boost to power, to 165bhp. But more importantly torque rose to 166lb/ft at 4200rpm. Standard equipment levels were raised, too, with anti-lock brakes, an automatic alarm system, automatic heating controls and electric seat adjustment included in the price.

Most attention was concentrated on the 944S, now called the 944S2. Its performance had been found lacking, being very little quicker than the standard 944 in its original form. To counteract this, there was a huge increase in capacity to 3.0 liters, achieved by taking in the 4mm bigger bore from the 944 and stretching the stroke from 78.9mm to 88mm. Racing experience led to a redesigned block, which was not only bigger but stiffer as well – yet weighed 15 percent less, with 33 percent less coolant. The changes, along with a new Bosch Motronic M2.1 engine management system, meant that top end output rose from 190 to 211bhp, and torque leapt from 170 to 207lb/ft at 4000rpm. To go with the extra power, Porsche in effect gave the S2 the body and suspension of the 220bhp Turbo. There was a stronger 5-speed gearbox: 4-piston, fixed-caliper vented disk brakes; anti-roll bars; and wider, 7 or 8in, forged alloy wheels fitted with 205/55 or 225/50 tires respectively. From the Turbo came the revised nose, lower rear spoiler and underbody treatment too, bringing the Cd down from 0.35 to 0.33. And the standard specification included those items mentioned above for the 944.

Since the S2 was now coming perilously close to the Turbo in terms of performance, the latter too was revised. The engine capacity stayed at 2.5

Above: A 944S in full flight – it's capable of over 140mph.

Left: The 944 mechanical lay-out, with the engine at the front and the transmission at the rear, joined by a torque tube.

Above right: The 1989 line-up, with a 944, an S2, a Turbo and a Cabriolet.

Right: The 944's interior is pure Porsche in both looks and function.

Far right: The 944S2 twin-cam, 3-liter, 16-valve engine.

liters, but the output became 250bhp by using the bigger turbocharger and higher boost settings mentioned earlier. Drawing from experience with the Turbo Cup series, there was a stronger 5-speed gearbox with an external cooler, a limited slip differential as standard, 928S4-type brakes, and special, forged, wheels, 7Jx16 with 225/50 tires up front, 9Jx16 with 245/45s at the rear.

The current 944 range is a far cry from the 2-liter 924 of 1975. Gone is the idea of 'The People's Porsche.' The range has been lifted into the higher price brackets, out of reach of the VW Corrados and Mazda RX7s, but in so doing Porsche have added considerable performance. In fact, there's no doubt that if you want to get from A to B in a hurry, any one of the new 944s will suffice. Chances are, its performance and roadholding will be far in excess of

anything anyone can put in its way, or that any sane driver could use in every-day motoring. With this comes considerable prestige, and with it all traces of the 'up-market Audi' syndrome have disappeared.

Mention has been made here of the 928. Speaking strictly chronologically, it should have been brought into the story at the very beginning of the chapter, since it was in the minds of the Porsche management, and on paper, before the 924 was started. But its position in the Porsche model heirarchy is such that it must be treated as a totally separate entity, and a car of equal if not greater importance.

The 928 was conceived at one of the most dramatic moments in Porsche's history. They had been working flat out on the VW EA266 project, a potential Beetle replacement with the engine tucked under the back seat. On

1 October 1971 Leiding replaced Lotz at VW – and promptly cancelled the project as he had strong ideas of his own.

The EA266 project was important to Porsche for another reason: it offered the potential for a new, small, VW-based, cheap Porsche as well. And suddenly that future disappeared.

By now, too, Dr Ernst Fuhrmann had taken over the reins from Ferry Porsche, and one of his and his team's first decisions was to decide the future model policy. They went to the other extreme.

First, the car would have a large, relatively slow revving engine, in which refinement and smoothness would take precedence over power per liter. For years they had avoided head-on clashes with Mercedes-Benz and BMW with their coupes, but with Porsches growing ever more expensive anyway, they could see that they could take a share of the costly, luxury market. They would aim for the more mature, discerning buyer who did not necessarily want spine-tingling performance or a boy-racer image.

As with the 924, noise, emissions and safety regulations were beginning to dominate automotive design at the time too. Nobody quite knew exactly in which direction these impending laws would move – except that they would be more stringent. All the points began to indicate that the new car would

have to conform to commonly accepted configurations. This meant a front mounted engine, water cooling, and rear wheel drive – similar constraints, as mentioned previously, would define the layout of the 924. But in the 928 and 924 Porsche would be setting the seeds for their production models for the 1980s and later, perhaps.

The decision to make the 928, and the broad concept, were thrashed out in a remarkably short time. It was to appeal to the sybaritic, but it would most definitely still be a Porsche. In fact it would also be the very first production Porsche that was all-Porsche from the ground up. The 356 had initially used VW components, the 911 carried over some 356 components. The 928 started with a blank sheet.

Initially a 3.5-liter V6 was considered, but it turned out to be too high,

Above left: The 944 Lux with 'telephone dial' wheels, which weren't widely applauded.

Left: In Porsche tradition the 944's cockpit is beautifully finished, even if the color choice is a little odd.

Above: The 1984 Porsche 928S2 looked too much like its earlier sisters for comfort – a little more distinction was needed.

Right: The 928's rear light clusters are deep inset inside the one-piece polyurethane rear bumper.

Above: Spot the difference (license plates apart) – one is a standard 928, the other an S. The rubbing strip on the S gives the game away.

Left: The raised headlamps on the 928 give it a rather quizzical, pop-eyed look.

Above right: Slotted wheels, a rubbing strake and small rear spoiler – no question that it's an S.

thanks in part to a 60 degree V angle. Eventually a 4474cc V8 was chosen.

Porsche were naturally *au fait* with state-of-the-art engineering, but the end result in the V8 was Porsche engineering at its best. All major castings were in light alloy. There were single overhead camshafts per bank, operating inclined valves in a wedge head via hydraulic tappets: drive to the camshafts was via a toothed rubber belt. With Bosch K-Jetronic fuel injection it produced 240bhp at 5250rpm.

Like the 924, and again for weight balance reasons, the transmission was at the back, but, unlike the smaller car, the gearbox was ahead of the final drive, between the back seats. Five speed manual or Daimler-Benz's three speed auto boxes were the alternatives.

The suspension at front and rear also broke with Porsche tradition. There were twin wishbones, coil springs and telescopic dampers at the front, and a unique system at the back. Tires were Pirelli P7s, braking by ventilated disks all round, and steering by power assisted rack and pinion.

Naturally the shape of the monocoque bodyshell had to reflect Porsche thinking. Tony Lapine and his team set to work. Like the 924, the bumper was the most prominent feature of the nose, with intakes tucked underneath. Like the 924, too, the shape was all large diameter curves, with not a sharp edge in sight. Unlike the 924, though, the rear window didn't wrap around. Curved, narrow, triangular three-quarter windows appeared at the side, their front edges following the sharp forward rake of the door windows and B pillars. And at first sight the car didn't appear to have any bumpers at all: in fact they were covered in a flexible polyurethane plastic, color-coded to the car. The result at the rear was a bare, bulbous expanse with insets for the tail lights and license plate. Another discussion point was that the headlamps were recessed in the hood, electrically operated to flip up when required, in the manner of the Lamborghini Miura.

The 928 was announced at Geneva on 16 March 1977. Even with experience from the 924, it was like no other Porsche ever before. Traditionalists, brought up on 911 and looking for a super version, condemned it as being too slow – even with 4.5 liters it wasn't as quick as a 911, even an unblown one, on acceleration, and there wasn't much difference in top speed. And it was thirstier. Compared to its rivals, some said it was too sporty, by which they meant it didn't have the refinement of a Mercedez-Benz or a Jaguar: compared to a 911, it was too soft. And yet it was voted 'Car of the Year' in 1978 and it was one of Porsche's best launches ever.

The euphoria was short-lived, though. That lack of performance rankled, especially among Porscheophiles, so it wasn't *too* surprising when, in August 1978, an additional model, called the 928S, was announced. With a marginal increase in capacity to 4.7 liters plus a more sporty cam profile, power rose to a nice round 300bhp at 5900rpm, and torque to 282lb/ft at 4500rpm. To go with the extra poke there was a discreet spoiler under the nose and another around the base of the rear window, rubbing strakes down the side and flat-faced wheels with peripheral slots in place of the 'telephone dials' of the standard car.

Above: Visually much as before, but the 1985 928S Series 2 featured a new fuel-injection system and slightly more power.

Left: A very full 928S4 engine bay, not surprising since it contained a 5-liter V8, four overhead camshafts and 32 valves.

Above right: With its wide center tunnel and wraparound facia plus full leather trim, this Porsche cocoons its occupants in luxury.

Right: It says much for the 928's aerodynamics that a massive rear spoiler isn't required.

The result of these changes turned the 928S into a real belter, with a maximum speed of 156mph compared to the standard model's 140mph. That was a bit more like it.

The 928S took over as the best seller in the range, to such an extent that the standard 928 was dropped in 1982. The next year the Bosch K-Jetronic fuel injection was replaced by the more modern hot-wire LH Jetronic system, which gave rise to slightly more power – 310bhp – and torque – 295lb/ft – not to mention a new name, the Series 2 (fortunately shortened to 928S2). Naturally performance rose too, but more importantly, with the closer engine control offered by the new electronics, fuel consumption was improved as well. ABS became standard.

It was not surprising that the S2 was followed by the S3 in 1985. What *was* surprising was that it was launched in the United States, and was exclusive to that market. Furthermore, it had a paper specification which had enormous appeal for the European market. The bore was taken out to a full 100mm, to give a capacity of 5 liters, while sitting on each bank of the V8 was a twin-

cam, 16-valve head. What would have had less appeal was the fact that it gave 'only' 288bhp. But this only happened when fitted with a catalysor. The 928S2 in American form only gave 234bhp, and it was the first engine to follow Porsche's intention to make all power units give the same output no matter where they were sold. *That* was the significance of it: no longer did the Americans and Japanese have to suffer any loss of power because of emission controls. On top of that, it was fairly obvious that the Europeans, led by Germany where the Green Party was particularly strong, would eventually have to fall into line on emissions as well.

When the 32-valve, 5-liter engine became available in Europe in the S4, in the middle of 1986, power was up to 320bhp at 6000rpm, little more than the European-spec S3, but 32bhp more than the original American-spec S3s. Torque was up to a stump-pulling 317lb/ft at 3000rpm. In addition Porsche tweaked the aerodynamics, with a more rounded nose which included an integral front spoiler and in which the cooling ducts were opened and closed by electronic servo motors. At the rear there was a more prominent spoiler, standing proud of the bodywork. That it worked was indisputable, but it looked like a bolt-on goodie bought from an accessory shop. The net result of these changes was a reduction in the Cd from 0.38 to 0.34, which had a marked effect on top speed. When they tested one, *Autocar* recorded a maximum of 160mph, and a 0-60mph of 6.2 sec (not to mention a 0-100mph time of 15.2 sec). What really puts these figures into context was that they were taken with an automatic version . . . In America, Al Holbert, head of Porsche's racing efforts in America, took a manual to Bonneville and flew across the salt flats at 171mph. Not bad for 'The Old Man's Porsche.'

Before finishing the 928 story, and that of the road-going Porsches to date, there is one rather special 928 that is worth mentioning. In 1984, Ferry Porsche was presented with a one-off, 4-seater 928 for his 75th birthday. It was 10in longer than standard, the extra length appearing in the wheelbase to give more rear seat legroom, and the roof line was extended into a semi-station wagon shape for additional head room. Back in 1987, at a press conference, Peter Schutz, when asked if it would ever see production, gave a firm 'no comment.' Could it be possible yet?

Taking to the Tracks

Porsche and competition are synonymous. Almost from the moment the first customers climbed into their little, low-slung coupes they were rarin' to go. Since 1950 barely a day, a week or a month has gone by without Porsches winning something somewhere, to such an extent that at times the company has been accused of overkill.

Porsche's sporting life can be divided roughly into five periods. There were the early days, the 1950s, with the 356-based cars. This was followed by the roadable, Carrera-engined machines. In the 1960s the mid-engined sports/racers slowly began to dominate the non-single-seater scene, culminating in the 917s. The 1970s can be classified as the (Fuhrmann Philosophy) 911/930 era, and the 1980s as Group C domination with the 956s and 962s.

The first recorded win by a Porsche was on 11 July 1948, when Herbert Kaes took the very first 356, the open mid-engined car, to a class win in a round the houses race at Innsbruck. That was more of a taster than anything else, since it wasn't until 1950 that success began to be noted. Prince Joachim zu Furstenberg, co-driven by Count Konstantin Berckheim, won the 1100cc class in the Swedish Rally of the Midnight Sun, the ladies award going to Countess Cecilia Koskull in a Gmünd coupe. Later Rudolf Sauerwein and Count von der Muhle-Eckart won their class and came second overall in the Interlaken International rally – the titled and Porsches seemed to go well together! In fact both motorcars and fuel were strictly rationed commodities in those post-war years in Europe, and it was usually only the rich, the famous and the upper crust who could indulge in such frivolity as motor sport.

With production getting under way at Stuttgart in 1950, it wasn't until 1951 that Porsches began to appear in any number on the tracks. Undoubtedly the most famous Porsche win that year was in the 1100cc class at Le Mans.

With alloy bodies and narrower roofs, the Gmünd cars were lighter and more streamlined than the Stuttgart cars, two reasons for using them in competition. For Le Mans they were further modified with louvered panels

over the rear side windows, fairings beneath nose and tail, and spats over the wheel arches. The 1086cc engines had been developed to give 46bhp on the fuel available. All this was enough to give the singleton entry, driven by Veuillet and Mouche, a top speed of almost exactly 100mph, and that famous class win.

1951 also saw the introduction of both the 1300cc and roller-bearing 1500cc engines, both given a baptism of fire.

The first was in June, in an extraordinary event, the Baden-Baden rally. This called for entrants to check in at as many controls as possible in a given time. To overcome the problem of American-imposed 50mph speed limits (sound familiar?) Porsche loaned their experimental license plates to the en-

Previous pages: One of the most famous RSKs ever, chassis number 718005, which finished third at Le Mans in 1958 and actually won the Targa Florio in 1959, driven by Jean Behra.

Left: Predecessor of all the racing Spyders, one of the Glockler Specials with mid-mounted engine.

Below left: In the early days rallying played a major part in Porsche activities – this is Mme Gilberte Thirion in the 1953 Alpine.

Right: A foretaste of things to come, with a 356 taking part in the 1964 Monte Carlo rally – 911s would win it later.

Below: The von Neumann roadster racer, made from a cut-down Gmund coupe, was a very successful machine in West Coast American racing.

trants who included Prince Zu Leiningen, Count Berckheim and a name that would figure prominently in Porsche history, Richard von Frankenberg, which allowed them to run flat out. The 1300s averaged 75mph for the 30 hours, with a fuel consumption of about 24mpg.

The 1500 made its bow in the infamous, car-breaking Liège-Rome-Liège rally. Two lightweight cars were entered, one an 1100cc for Huschke von Hanstein, (another name that would become famous in Porsche lore) and Petermax Muller, and the 1500, officially labelled a 1300 as the bigger unit hadn't been publicly announced, for Paul von Guilleaume and Count von der Muhle. Von Hanstein came second in class, while von Guilleaume not only won his class but was placed third overall.

The fourth significant event in 1951 was a record-breaking session at Mon-

thléry. Three cars took part, two Gmünd coupes with an 1100 and the new 1500cc engines respectively, and a little sports/racing open two-seater that would have special significance in later years. It was built by Walter Glöckler, a VW dealer from Frankfurt, and was naturally powered by Porsche, but with the engine reversed so that it was in front of the rear wheels with the gearbox behind.

Numerous records were taken. The 1100 coupe broke the 500 mile, 1000km and six hour records at 100.3mph, 101.4mph and 101.1mph. The Glöckler car took the same distance records for the open car class at 116.6mph, 115.3mph and 114.35mph. But most effort was concentrated on the 1500 coupe, and in spite of the loss of all gears but third, took the 72 hour record at 94.66mph. It was this car that appeared proudly on Porsche's stand at Paris a few days later.

In America, the irrepressible Max Hoffman won his class at the Mt Equinox, Vermont, hill climb on 28 October 1951 so convincingly in a cabriolet that Briggs Cunningham promptly bought one and took a first in class at Palm Springs Lake, Florida, on 8 December. Both were 1500s.

Three cars were prepared for the 1952 Le Mans race, two 1100s and a 1500: the von Hanstein/Muller car retired, the 1500 was disqualified, but an 1100, with the same drivers as the year before, Veuillet and Mouche, won its class. In the Liège-Rome-Liège event Porsche almost swamped the results, with Polensky/Schluter first overall in a Gmünd coupe, a newcomer to the Porsche game called Hans Herrmann, co-driving for a Belgian, Stasse, coming in third and von Guilleaume and Scheube fourth.

The technique for cornering early Porsches had a name in German: *wischen*, or wipe. Basically the idea is similar in some respects to modern rally driving methods, in that oversteer is provoked by the driver first, the tail of the car then being controlled by the throttle and a wild sawing of the steering wheel. Get out of sequence, though, and you would execute what aviators call a 'flick-roll . . . .

Between 1950 and 1953, Walter Glöckler had built and raced a series of light, open, Porsche-powered specials, the first two of which were mid-engined. Glöckler was very successful with these, receiving advice and special parts from Porsche who recognized the value of his wins. Influenced by the success of the Glöckler cars, realizing that the Gmünd coupes were becoming out-dated, and that sports/racing cars such as those produced by Gordini, OSCA and others were becoming more specialized, Ferry Porsche decided in 1952 to build sports/racers.

The car was called the type 550. The basis was a simple ladder-type frame, with the usual steering, brakes and torsion bar front suspension. As the engine was placed amid-ships the rear suspension was turned through 180 degrees as well, with the transverse torsion bars in the rearmost cross-tube of the frame. The engine was that from the 1500 Super, but tuned to give near to 100bhp on alcohol fuel and a 12.5:1 compression ratio. The bodyshell was of light alloy and very sleek, with rather protuberant head-lamps and contoured fenders. Two body styles were in fact designed, one open, the other closed.

The first one to be completed ran on 31 May 1953 in the Eifel Races at the Nurburgring – and promptly won, making it a first time out winner. But this was just a trial for Le Mans.

Two cars were prepared, detuned to run on gasoline in which form they gave 78bhp. Streamlined hardtops were fitted, which deafened, cooked and gave the drivers claustrophobia, but which also increased their top speed. The driver pairings were Helm Glöckler, Walter's cousin, and Hans Herrmann

Above: A name famous in Porsche folk-lore, Carrera Panamericana. Here Kling (in car), von Hanstein (left) and Herrmann pose before the start of the 1953 event.

Left: The original 550s were fitted with a roof for better streamlining on the long, fast Mulsanne straight at Le Mans.

Right: Claude Storez with his Carrera Speedster gave Porsche many rally wins in 1957, including the Lyons-Charbonnieres, where the car took a bit of a battering.

making his first sortie to Le Mans, with von Frankenberg and the talented Belgian journalist Paul Frère in the second car.

The two cars circulated consistently – within a lap of each other most of the time – and fast enough to win the class with ease, the honor going to von Frankenberg and Frère.

When Ferry Porsche decided to enter the sports/racing field more seriously it was obvious that pushrod engines had their limitations, and that twin overhead camshaft units were going to be *de rigeur* for success. Egged on by von Hanstein, who was by mid-1952 both competitions manager and head of public relations, he instituted the design of a new engine. The man he and Karl Rabe chose to design the new engine was Ernst Fuhrmann. From it was to stem, in later years, a bewildering array of engines, but all with the same theme.

It was, naturally, a flat four, of 1498cc. It featured a roller bearing crankshaft and a unique valve drive train. Other features included a classic hemispherical combustion chamber and twin plugs per cylinder.

To go with the new engine, the 550 was redesigned. The chassis was modified slightly, but the most important change was to the rear suspension, the torsion bars being repositioned in front of the axle. Komenda altered the body shape a little – not much, but enough to give the 550 a classically beautiful shape.

Two cars of the new shape were prepared for the Carrera Panamericana in 1953 in fact, and were driven by Herrmann and the 1952 overall winner (in a Mercedes-Benz), Karl Kling. Since the four-cam was not yet deemed raceworthy, they were fitted with 1500 pushrod engines, but both retired. However, Herrmann and the car he drove in 1953 took part in the Carrera again in 1954, this time fitted with a four-cam unit: he not only won his class but came in an astonishing third overall. 1954 was the last of these famous races, but the name was to live on in Porsche legend.

The first major sortie in 1954 of the four-cam 550 was the Mille Miglia on 1 May. Herrmann and Linge were entrusted with the new car, and finished a resounding sixth overall and first in class – in spite of a terrifying moment when

they had to race a train to a level crossing. By ducking their heads they just made it.

Le Mans, however, remained the focal point of Porsche's efforts in 1954. Four cars were prepared for Le Mans, three with the 1.5-liter four-cam engines and one with an 1100cc version of the same. The three bigger-engined cars all suffered from holed pistons, but the Stasse/Claes 1500 carried on, and when the main competition, the OSCAs, dropped out in the last hour, staggered across the line 12th overall and the only car left in its class. The 1.1-liter car was 14th and again the sole survivor in its class.

The 1.1 car was driven by Gustave Olivier and Zora Arkus Duntov of Ardun head and Corvette fame. In discussions with Duntov about handling, Bott was told about GM's skid-pan and the results that could be obtained from it. Bott soon after found a suitable open space, at Malmsheim, and introduced skid-pan work to Porsche: again, from such humble beginnings, the vast, complex Weissach test facility would be born, and a skid-pan would play a vital part in Porsche car development.

Customer 550s started appearing in late 1954, and were officially designated 550/1500RS – until Max Hoffman, not too enamored with numbers, suggested the model be called the 'Spyder.' From then on the name has always been used by Porsche to designate open, lightweight semi-racers or racers. In all, two 550s were sold in 1954, 63 in 1955 and 13 in 1956.

For the tragic 1955 Le Mans race, Porsche overcame the piston-burning propensity of the previous year, and finished 1-2 in the 1500cc class and 1-2 in the 1100cc class as well, the leading 1.5 car placing a splendid fourth overall as well. Drivers were Polensky and von Frankenberg.

Come 1956 and the 550 received its first major revision. The early cars' frames were regarded as rather whippy, and odd things could happen to the power outputs of the engine which were traced to the fact that the distributors were driven by the camshafts.

Officially called the 550A, but more usually known as the RS, the major change was a brand new chassis, which echoed the very first type 356 in that it was a space frame. The rear suspension too was modified but in a way that

Left: The Type 550 sold in some numbers to customers who raced them all over the world.

Below: The late, great, Graham Hill in a Carrera Abarth during the 1960 TT at Goodwood with signs of a 'coming-together.'

Right: Despite being made in relatively large numbers, few Spyders survive – this is one, preserved in immaculate condition and raced *con brio* by the Italian Corrado Cupellini.

broke with tradition. Gone was the simple swing axle, replaced by a low-pivot arrangement, with arms under the half shafts (which were therefore splined to accept length variations) to locate the wheels. The power output of the engine was increased. All in all, the 550A or RS was a much-modified machine: the handling was improved, thanks to the lighter but stronger chassis which overcame the ladder frame's whippiness, and the more sophisticated rear suspension, while it was faster too.

Its first appearance in April in the Mille Miglia resulted in retirement, but a month later Wolfgang von Trips and Umberto Maglioli finished fourth overall and first in class at the Nurburgring 1000kms, with Herrmann and von Frankenberg in sixth and second in class behind them.

However, 10 June 1956 saw the RS score one of Porsche's greatest wins until then, the first of a long line, in a race that, like the Carrera, would give its name to a Porsche model: the Targa Florio. Against the cream of the sports/racing cars and drivers (including Castellotti in a Monza Ferrari and Taruffi in a 300S Maserati) Umberto Maglioli drove single handed for nearly eight hours to take the checkered flag.

Development work on the 550A carried on over the winter of 1956/57, using the lessons that lightness and a smaller frontal area could be beneficial. The whole car was lowered and lightened and streamlined, with faired in headlamps. The front suspension was redesigned, too. The upper tubes which carried the torsion bars were placed in a V-shape, the point being at the bottom in the middle of the frame. With the bottom tube staying as it was, the result looked like the letter K – and the new car was instantly dubbed the RSK.

However, it was given a Porsche Type number, 718, and this generic numeral would cover not just the RSKs but its good-looking and powerful successors in sportscar, Formula 2 and Formula 1 races.

Below left: The RS60 with bigger windshield to meet new regulations.

Right: Dan Gurney in action in a 718 coupe during practice for the 1961 Nürburgring 1000kms.

must be corrected with a very gentle movement of the steering wheel: any sudden or violent movement throws the car out of control.'

That's as may be. To me, that day at Bridgehampton was one of the most exhilarating I've ever had, and the RSK one of the greatest cars I'll ever drive.

One of the advantages of the RSK was that the steering box was on the car's centerline, so that it could be relatively easily converted to a central driving position. Which is precisely what Porsche did for the Rheims F2 race two weeks after Le Mans in 1958. They took the Frère/Barth car which had placed fourth overall and first in the 1500cc class, adding rear wheel spats, a special tonneau cover over the cockpit and a wrap-around aero screen. Behra drove it, fins and all, and proved the point about streamlining by winning. At the Nürburgring in August a finless, spatless center-seater driven by Barth came second in the F2 section of the GP meeting, and sixth overall. But the competition from the open-wheeled cars was getting stiffer.

One other important RSK result came in October 1958 at the Los Angeles Times Grand Prix, the 'first major professional sportscar contest in post-war America,' as Karl Ludvigsen put it. Behra was placed fourth against strong, and much bigger-engined, opposition.

The FIA announced in late 1958 that, as from the 1961 season, Formula 1 would limit engine capacity to 1.5-liters, full-width bodywork would be banned, and a minimum weight limit of 1100lbs would be imposed. This gave Porsche food for thought: they had enormous experience with 1.5-liter engines, and a single-seater RSK might be competitive.

Thus the closed season between 1958 and 1959 saw the Porsche engineers and racing department concentrating on refining and obtaining more power from the RSK, and adding a single-seater program for F2, initially, but with F1 in mind, to their workload.

The F2/1 car project gathered momentum. The basis of the car was so close to the RSK that it was simply given the Type number 718/2. It used the RSK's four-cam engine and brakes, the torsion bar front suspension but the new wishbone rear, and the chassis was a simple space frame. It was covered by the bulky open-wheeled aluminum shell. However, the sheer width of the boxer engines meant that they could never match the English machines on frontal area, or lack of it.

The works 718/2 finished third at Rheims behind Herrmann and, to gain experience with this form of racing, was entered for a minor English event, the Kentish Trophy at Brands Hatch in August. Bonnier finished third and fourth in his heats. More significantly, and perhaps the reason for bringing the car over at all, was that Stirling Moss drove it a week later in trials at Goodwood. A car was offered to Rob Walker for Moss to drive on a semi-official basis in 1960, and this was accepted by Walker.

Thus 1960 saw a works team and the Rob Walker car contesting F2, while the RSKs were updated to meet the new sportscar regulations, which called for wider cockpits, bigger windshields, room for a 'suitcase' and spare wheel, and a production run of 100, the purpose being to make the cars more like real production machines. With blazing originality, the cars Porsche made to meet these regulations were called RS60s.

The first 718/2 went to the Walker equipe, the rest to the works team. They had a fairly eventful year: Moss was second at Brussels; Gendebien third at Pau. For the Solitude race all five of the 718/2s produced appeared, one of them with styling by Butzi Porsche. It had a squarer, more compact, neater body with an open tail, but was not a thing of beauty. Von Trips won the Solitude race in a Ferrari, though Herrmann was second. Porsche avenged themselves at the F2 German GP in July though, finishing first (Bonnier), second (von Trips – Ferrari had not attended the meeting), fourth (Graham Hill), fifth (Herrmann) and sixth (Barth). At Zeltweg, Moss, who had injured himself at Spa, returned to give Porsche a first, Bonnier followed this up with another on Ferrari's home ground at Modena, and the season came to a close with Moss winning a couple of races in South Africa. On the whole, Porsche's first forays into single-seaters were successful.

The RS60s maintained the winning ways of the RSKs. Bonnier and Herrmann won the Targa, Gendebien/Herrman won at Sebring, and Bonnier/Gendebien were third at the Nurburgring 1000kms. But, as in 1959, there was a blot on the landscape: Le Mans. The works cars had raised rear decks and side windows to lower aerodynamic drag – almost a 'Targa' top. Only one finished, in 11th position. The other four, two works, two private, RSKs dropped out. Fortunately, as ever, customer cars kept the name of Porsche in the winners circles, all over the globe.

So successful in private hands was the RS60, in fact, that Porsche carried on making it in 1961 as the RS61.

In 1960, however, a far-reaching decision had been made: to go ahead with a new engine which, in 1.5-liter form could take on the best the F1 opposition could offer, and in 2-liter form appear in sports cars. The final configuration was an air-cooled flat-eight. However the engine wouldn't be ready for the first season of the new 1.5-liter formula, so the 718/2 was redesigned.

With a new chassis the cars were slimmer and broke yet another Porsche tradition by using twin wishbone front suspension (gone at last were the VW-based trailing arms and torsion bars), either four or five speed boxes, and Kugelfischer mechanical fuel injection.

The new cars were an unmitigated disaster, in spite of the efforts of Bonnier and Gurney in particular to make them competitive. After the Dutch GP at Zandvoort, when it was clear that the new 718/2s were not competitive,

Ferry Porsche decided to drop them and revert to the 1960 cars – at least they were known and trusted. With them Gurney notched up three second places, at Rheims, Watkins Glen and Monza.

While offering sports RSKs to customers, and even suggestions and options for improvements to keep them competitive, Porsche made three specials for themselves for 1961. Two were coupes in which Butzi had taken a hand, with long, slim noses, large windshields, and roofs that were chopped off abruptly about a foot behind the cockpit. They were called simply 718 coupes, but the third, open, car was called the W-RS.

The W-RS's first outing was to the Targa, driven by Gurney and Bonnier. It finished second behind a Ferrari, but Moss and Graham Hill had led until the last lap when a loss of oil in the transmission put them out, a few miles from the finish. This car was a 1960 RS60 but fitted, as was the W-RS, with a 1966cc plain-bearing four-cylinder engine, forerunners of those for the Carrera 2.

At the Nürburgring the W-RS was 10th after engine troubles. For Le Mans, Porsche entered all three of the new models, both coupes and the W-RS, all with different engine capacities. Masten Gregory and Bob Holbert stroked the W-RS to fifth, with Barth and Herrmann two places behind in one of the coupes.

During 1960 and 1961, the Abarth-Carreras were up-holding Porsche GT honors. In 1960 one of these machines was Porsche's only official entry at Le Mans in the GT category, coming in 11th overall and first in class, while in 1961 Abarth-Carreras finished in the points in the Targa, at Le Mans, in the Paris 1000kms, and, driven by Gurney and Holbert, one came seventh over-all and – of course – first in class at Sebring in early 1962.

What is there to say about Porsche's F1 efforts in 1962? Problems arose fairly quickly. The new eight cylinder engine wasn't giving quite the hoped-for outputs in 1.5-liter form. However a new chassis was designed and built for it. To some extent this followed then-current practice, with a tubular space frame, wishbone suspension at either end and a smaller, slimmer, lighter body, akin to that Butzi had produced for the F2 car, reduced frontal area.

The car's first outing, after trials at the Malmsheim skid pan had shown that it could generate the highest cornering powers a Porsche had ever achieved, was at the Dutch Grand Prix on 20 May, 1962. To show what it was up against, the same race saw the Lotus 25 in its first race – a lean, ultra-light machine, powered by the Climax V8, whose major feature broke new ground, for it was the first of Colin Chapman's monocoques. At a stroke the Porsches – and the BRMs and Ferraris *et al* – were outdated.

The F1 car's finest hour came in France, at the Rouen-les-Essarts circuit, on 8 July. Gurney, helped by an astonishing attrition rate, won. It was the car's best performance, and because other, faster machines dropped out is no cause to belittle the car's achievement. A win is a win.

A win in the non-Championship Solitude GP a week later boosted Porsche aspirations again but from then on it became obvious that it was not really competitive, and before the end of the season Ferry Porsche called a halt to F1 participation.

Why did Porsche not pursue F1? There were a number of reasons. One was that it was costing far too much money: with the other competition cars at least some of the outgoings could be recouped by selling customer versions. It was taking up a lot of the engineers' time when there were other projects, such as the potential 356 replacement, to be attended to. The engine, though a good design, obviously needed more work on it just to keep up with the opposition, never mind get ahead. There were the internal politics. But perhaps the one reason that has never been voiced publicly is that Porsche were really out of their depth in what was to them a whole new ball game, a very specialized form of motor racing. Their field was fast, rugged, reliable sportscars and long-distance racing.

This was emphasized by their other efforts in 1962 and 1963. After Le Mans in 1961 a 718 coupe and the W-RS were rebuilt and re-engined with the 2-liter versions of the eight-cylinder engine. In contrast to the F1 version, the sportscar engine seemed to suffer relatively few birth pangs.

Some ten months after Le Mans, and before the F1 car had appeared, the eight-cylindered 718 and W-RS were entered for the Targa Florio by Count Volpi's Scuderia SSS Republica de Venezia. The W-RS was in the usual Porsche silver, but the coupe was finished in the most hideous flat red. The W-RS crashed out of the race, but the red coupe struggled on brakeless to come home third.

Porsche relied again on these cars for 1963. They were rebuilt once more, this time with wishbone front suspension, and weight was cut by using glass-fiber panelling, while the latest engine modifications were applied. This time the coupe driven by Bonnier and Carlo Abate pressed home to a Targa win at record speed.

Both the coupe and W-RS retired at Le Mans, but the W-RS went on to a great and glorious career in other spheres. It was raced for a while in America, and then returned for Edgar Barth to use in the European hill climb championship, which he succeeded in winning two years in a row, 1963 and 1964. The car was entered in the 1964 Targa again, with Graham Hill and Jo Bonnier driving, but retired with half shaft trouble. So well known was this car in the Porsche competitions department that it was nicknamed *Grossmutter*, or grandmother. Edgar Barth died in 1964, and *Grossmutter* was never raced again.

Above: The 1962 F1 single-seater wasn't competitive enough compared to its British contemporaries.

Left: The RSK, chassis number 718005, which the author drove at Bridgehampton race track near New York.

Right: The Rob Walker/Stirling Moss F2 car being built at Stuttgart.

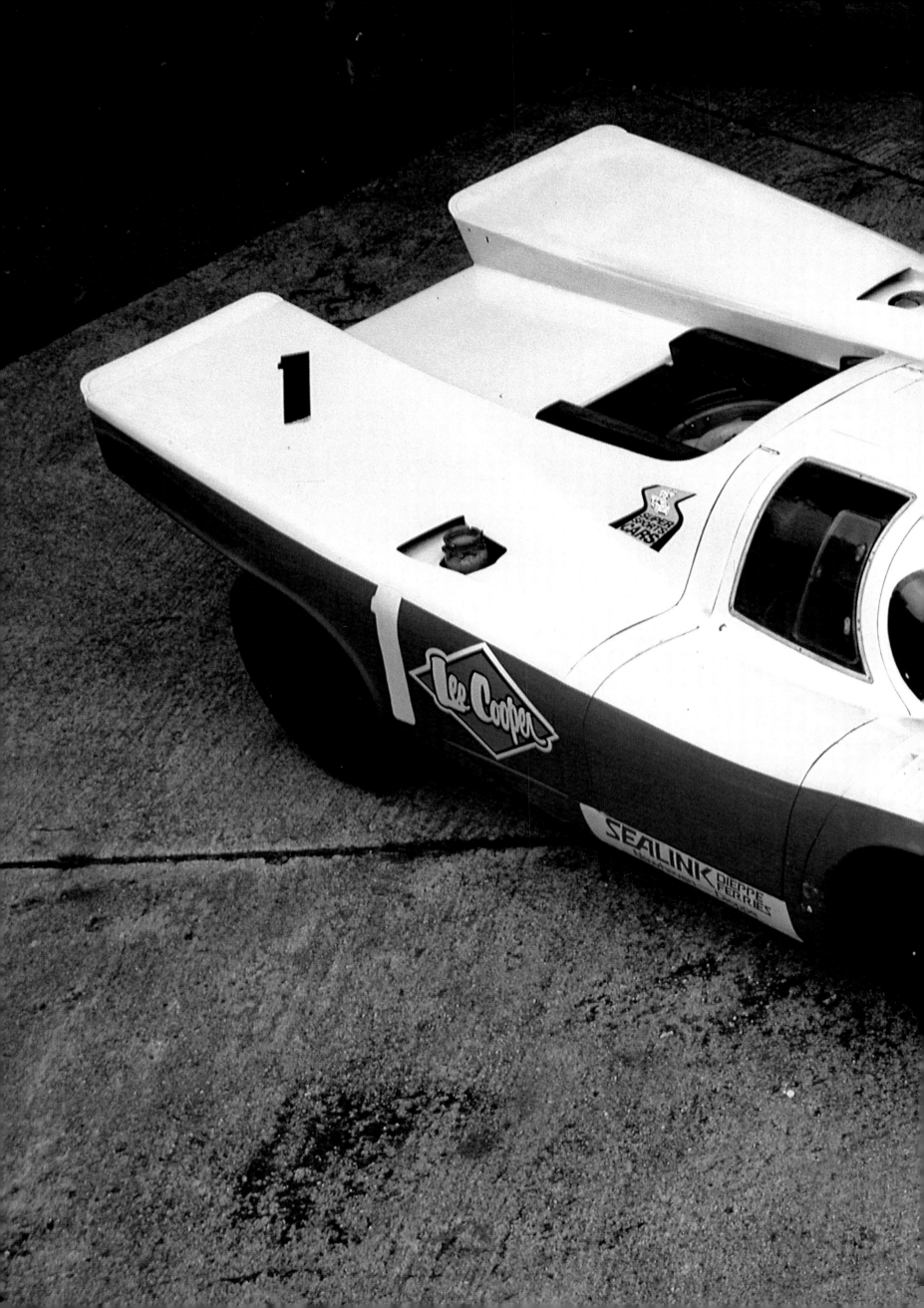

The Road to Glory

The decade from 1963 to 1973 could be called the period during which Porsche grew up – or rather, during which their engines grew up. At the start the largest engine was of 2 liters, and the most powerful produced about 250bhp: by the end capacity had risen to over 5 liters, and power was a staggering 1100bhp, the most powerful racing units ever for track use. It could also be called the time of the 9-series, for it saw the 904, 906, 907, 908, 910 and 917 racers and the beginnings of the competition 911.

The early 1960s had been exhausting both in terms of cash and manpower for Porsche. There was the F1 program, initial development and design of the 911, not to mention outside contracts. And with the new 911, it was unthinkable that a Carrera equivalent could be missing from the line-up. Von Hanstein was pushing hard for something to replace the Abarth-Carreras, or GTLs as they were officially known. The RSs, RSKs and their derivatives were keeping the name of Porsche ahead on the tracks, but Porsche needed a new customer race car.

Thus the decision was taken in the winter of 1962/1963 to go ahead with a new GT model. It was called the 904.

One of the parameters laid down was that it was to use the engine and transmission from the up-coming 911 (or 901 as it was numbered internally at Porsche) but rotated 180 degrees so that the power unit was in front of the rear wheels, thus following the RS, RSK and 718 design – and cashing in on the image that such a layout could confer. It would be aimed at the 2-liter GT Championship, and therefore 100 would have to be made for homologation purposes.

In the end, the 911's six-cylinder engine wasn't ready in time, so the four-cylinder, four-cam engine from the Carrera 2 and Abarth-Carrera was used instead. The five-speed transmission was, however, that of the 911.

What really set the 904 apart was the body, a fiberglass affair which was bonded to the chassis for added stiffness. It was the work of Butzi Porsche, and was one of, if not the, most inspired of his works. The front section – nose and cockpit – had some affinity with the 718 coupe, but the tail curved gently around the wheels to an abrupt cut-off. Touches, such as the way the outer edge of the hood formed the inner edge of the headlamp covers, the beautiful curvature of the rear part of the roof, and the way the doors took part of the roof with them when they opened, all added up to a car that looked beautiful yet entirely purposeful.

And it was to be a production car. The standard color scheme was silver outside, blue inside, it was officially called the Carrera GTS, and the first car was delivered on 17 January 1964.

Its first race was at Sebring in March 1964. In fact five lined up, and the Lake Underwood/Briggs Cunningham car finished ninth overall and first in the 3-liter prototype class, since the homologation papers hadn't become effective.

The real sensation of the year, though, came on 26 April, when a 904, driven by Colin Davis and Antonio Pucci, won the Targa! What's more it was followed home by another 904.

The 904 had a highly successful career, including the 2-liter GT championship in 1964. Perhaps the other most historic, and certainly unusual, successes was a fighting second – in the 1965 Monte Carlo rally! It proved to be a genuine race *and* road car – but it was to be the last such Porsche.

The company themselves modified a few to take up the cudgels in the prototype stakes where the 718 and W-RS left off. Eight-cylinder 904s were entered for the Targa and Le Mans in 1964, but retired in both (though standard 904s finished 7th, 8th, 10th, 11th and 12th at the Sarthe circuit that year). Through 1965 the 904 upheld Porsche colors honorably.

There was even a Spyder version, and it was this that was fitted with the engine that should have gone into the 904 in the first place – the flat six, single overhead camshaft (per bank) unit destined for the 911.

For the Spyders, the plastic bodywork was reduced to the bare minimum to cover the mechanicals, with additional strengthening to the frame to make up for any lack of stiffness. Wider and wider tires were fitted – this was the time when tire widths grew greater almost every day – the bodywork being suitably widened each time to accommodate them.

However, the 904 Spyders were significant in more than one respect. In 1965, Ferdinand Piëch took over in charge of research and development, with Helmuth Bott as his deputy. He was working his way up the Porsche ladder, and the Spyder was one step.

The 904 Spyder with box-section chassis was not a great success against Scarfiotti in the Ferrari. In the middle of 1965 Piëch and his team decided that, to make a dent in the Italian's hill-climb dominance, a brand new car was needed – in a hurry, too. The starting point was quite literally the wheels: the Ferrari was on 13 inchers, *à la* Formula 1 cars of the period, and Piëch wanted a set, and quickly. He bought them from Team Lotus at the German Grand Prix at the end of July, complete with hubs, brakes and suspension uprights. The chassis of the 904 was rejected in favor of a multi-tubular space frame, the engine was a 2-liter flat eight, and the bodywork as skimpy as possible. The car was rushed to completion and taken to Ollon-Villars in Switzerland for its debut on 29 August, barely two months after the decision to go

Previous pages: Seldom in the history of motor racing has there been a racer to match the sheer glory and presence of the awesome Porsche 917. This example is still raced in historic events.

Below, left and right: The 904, or Carrera GTS, was one of Butzi Porsche's most beautiful cars. It was a heavy but strong and reliable machine whose forte was long-distance endurance events in the GT classes. In shorter, straightforward races it couldn't keep up with the lightweight Lotuses and Elvas.

Right: A 904 at Le Mans, 1965 – but it's a test day, hence the lack of spectators.

Left: The rare hill-climb Type 909, Mitter aboard, at Gaisberg – it anticipated future trends.

Below left: The Herrmann/Linge 906 leads one of the Ferraris at Le Mans, 1966.

Right: Not all Porsche 906s were white – this is an Italian entry in the Targa Florio of 1967. Note lack of rear window.

ahead. Unfortunately it didn't win, but was from then on known as the Ollon-Villars car. This car is one of the most significant in Porsche racing history.

With the 906, the 904's replacement, Ferdinand Piëch set Porsche racing cars off on another tack. Gone was the 904 box-section chassis, replaced by a space-frame based on that of the Ollon-Villars car. The suspension was, however, more or less that of the 904, while the engine was that of the 911. In this installation it produced some 210bhp at 8000rpm. The transaxle too was basically 911, with a load of optional transmission ratios.

The body was quite distinctive. The nose was incredibly low, with high flared wheelarches, the rear was a vast plastic window, into which were let ventilation louvers, and the tail finished off with a vestigial spoiler. The headlamp coverings were distinctive for they curved around under the bottom of the front fenders. The doors opened gull-wing fashion.

The design of the 906 had started in the fall of 1965, and if it was to meet the FIA's regulations for the 1966 Sports car category 50 would have to be made. By January 1966 all had been sold, it was announced to the public in the same month (and was given the official name of 'Carrera 6') and homologation came through on 1 May as a Group 4 sportscar.

The 906 too had its share of successes, including the almost inevitable win in the Targa Florio. For Le Mans the cars were fitted with fuel injection (which put them in the prototype category) and long tails, which in practice showed a remarkable propensity for lift-off. Small trim tabs cured this, and one of the injected cars, driven by Jo Siffert and Colin Davis, finished fourth overall behind the massive 7-liter Ford GT40 Mk 2s and won the Index of Performance, based on speed and fuel consumption.

The 906 set the pattern for the next four years, and indeed for a long time to come. A space frame, tunnel-tested aero-dynamics, and a multi-cylindered engine would be seen in the next six pure racers.

In 1966 the 911 emerged as a rally car. Vic Elford gave Porsche another of their greatest victories in 1968, by winning the Monte Carlo rally in a 911 – and the day after it finished, flew off to America for a race the next week at Daytona. He was one of the drivers that won that event in yet another new racing car, the 907. Some week! Those years between 1966 and 1969 saw one of Porsches most hectic development periods, with new, modified, refined, or just plain different models appearing at almost every race.

First in pecking order if not in numerical sequence came the 910. This essentially took the 906's space frame, which could take either the 2-liter six or the 2.2-liter eight. From the Ollon-Villars car came the idea of the 13-inch wheels shod with fatter tires, while both the 906 and the Ollon-Villars car provided ideas for the suspension, though with new geometry and components. The body aped the 906's, but the smaller wheels meant that the front wheel arches could be reduced in size, to the benefit of forward vision. The doors too opened in the normal fashion, hinged at the front, while the large plastic

rear window disappeared, and the small piece of roof between the tops of the doors could be removed if necessary to make a Spyder.

The 910 was introduced at the end of 1966 but 1967 was the year of the 910. They finished first, second and third in the Targa, filling the same three positions at the Nürburgring 1000kms and at Mugello. They were also placed in various other races. Following Porsche's usual procedure at the time, 28 910s were produced, all as works cars, but were sold off in the middle of 1967 since there was yet *another* model taking off.

This was the 907. Like the 906 and 910, it too was evolutionary, being based on the 910 chassis and running gear, but clothed in an astonishing new body shape. Its initial primary purpose was to win Le Mans in 1967, and for this reason the first 907s had bodies that had been finely sculptured in the Stuttgart wind tunnel. The nose was shorter and less pointed, but the tail was an incredibly long sweeping shape, curving up over the rear wheels and then back to a narrow, horizontal slit. Reducing frontal area, difficult to do with the ever-increasing width of racing tires, was achieved by making the roof much narrower: it was fronted by a vast, swept round windshield, and backed by a long tapering rear window incorporating air ducts.

With the fiberglass of the bodies barely set, two 907Ls (L standing for *Langheck*, or long tail) were rushed to Le Mans for the practice days in April. Unfortunately the aerodynamics were far from being *au point*, and the cars were a real handful along the fast Mulsanne straight. Work around the rear end was required before the cars would be race ready.

It would be nice to report that the 907L won at Le Mans, but one retired and the other finished fifth overall, taking the Index of Performance for its speed capability and 2-liter engine.

At the press launch of the 1968 season models in December 1967, von Hanstein showed a variant of the 907L, the short-tailed 907 whose rear end owed more than a little to the hill-climb Spyder version of the 910 cars, and which was rather more practical on tighter, twisty circuits.

The 907 started its brief but illustrious career in 1968 with an amazing 1-2-3 finish at Daytona, on 3/4 February the three 907Ls crossing the line abreast, the actual winning car being driven by no less than five drivers at various times during the 24 hours. All the 907s produced were now fitted with the 2.2-liter four-cam engine that could trace its origins back to the abortive GP car.

23 March 1968 saw the short-tail 907s first outing – and first win, with Siffert/Herrmann coming in first and Elford/Neerpasch second. This was followed by yet another Targa win in a short-tailed car driven by Elford and Maglioli. But that was the 907's swan song, for – although it was entered in a few more races with reasonable placings – there was yet *another* model ready to pounce: the 908.

It would not be too far from the truth to say that the *raison d être* of the

908 came about because of Ford's overwhelming win at Le Mans in 1967 with the massive, 7-liter, Mk IVs. Perhaps in a fit of pique, or because they could see mega-buck companies like Ford trouncing everything in sight, the FIA announced in mid-1967 that, as from 1968, the regulations for the Sports Car Manufacturers' Championship would limit engine capacity to 3 liters for the prototypes in Group 6 and 5 liters for the Group 4 cars, of which fifty had to have been built: this was so that those people with Lolas and GT40s could still compete.

The new rules appealed to Porsche. They had the building blocks: the 907 had shown that, even in 2.2-liter form, it was highly competitive. But the ex-F1 engine couldn't be enlarged, and was in any case a complex and expensive unit. On the other hand, there was a twin overhead cam conversion available on the 901/911 engine. It could be expanded by the addition of two more cylinders . . .

And that was more or less what they did. Thus the 908, one of the most illustrious Porsches, was, like its predecessors, evolutionary rather than revolutionary. It was also the most powerful engine ever made by Porsche up till then, producing a conservative 310bhp when it was tested in December 1967, but this had risen to 350bhp when the car first appeared.

The 908 made its first appearance at the annual Le Mans practice days in April. Like the 907L, it was far from stable on the fast Mulsanne straight. Its first race was at Monza, where two were entered and neither finished. Two more 908Ks (K for Kurzheck, or short-tail) appeared for the Nürburgring 1000kms, and the Siffert/Elford car won.

For Le Mans, postponed that year to September, Porsche fielded four 908Ls, modified in the light of experience, with long, fixed fins over the rear wings, carrying at their extremities a fixed wing whose ends were moveable flaps, suspension-operated. By now the engines had been opened up from the initial capacity of 2921cc to 2996cc as well, and gave 350bhp. Only one survived, however, delayed by long pit stops, eventually finishing third. All in all, 1968 was not a brilliant season for the 908s.

When January 1969 came around, Porsche showed their 908 line-up, now consisting of Ls, Ks and a new model, the Spyder: as its name suggests the Spyder was the open version of the 908. They also had a new team manager, Rico Steinmann: Huschke von Hanstein was relegated once more to Press Officer.

The Spyder took advantage in a rule change for prototypes with engines up to 3 liters: they were no longer required to have a minimum ground clearance, windshield height, or room for a 'suitcase' or spare wheel. The Spyder looked like what it was — a decapitated 908K. It was called the 908/02.

Undoubtedly 1969 was the year of the 908, though it started badly when all five 908Ls retired at Daytona on the first two days of February. At Sebring, too, late in March, the best a 908 could do was a third, the car being a Spyder having its first outing.

But from then on things could hardly go wrong. Spyders took the first three places at the BOAC 500 at Brands Hatch, and then shattered the opposition in the Targa, taking the first *four* places. In the meantime a 908L had won at Monza, and another later won at Spa, in spite of the longer car's unpredictability and the drivers' dislike of it.

After the Nürburgring, in which Spyders filled the first five places, a 908L covered itself in unbelievable glory — by coming second at Le Mans. The finish that year will go down in history, for in the final hour Herrmann in the 908 and Ickx in the GT40 fought it out tooth and nail, with the younger Belgian just pipping the veteran of 13 Le Mans races. It was an epic race that can still generate considerable feeling in those who were there.

Finally, at Watkins Glen, Spyders again took the first three places — but in the last round that year another raucous bellow was heard from the tail of the winning Porsche, that of a flat 12 . . .

The 908, no matter how brilliant, was soon to be overshadowed and the car that was going to do it was the great 917.

When the FIA arbitrarily decreed that for the Sports Car Manufacturers' Championship prototypes would be limited to 3 liters and 'production' cars, of which fifty had to be built, could run to 5 liters, there was, not unnaturally, an outcry. Smaller companies couldn't hope to make that many: at a meet-

Below left and bottom left: The 908's 3-liter, 375bhp flat-eight engine, later superceded by the 917's flat-twelve and the all-conquering *Panzerwagen* into which it was fitted, creating the 917/30 which dominated Can-Am racing.

Right: Le Mans 1969, and the race that made the 908 immortal, with Herrmann finishing second to Ickx's Ford by mere seconds.

Below: A 908-3 in the 1970 version of the race that Porsche made their own, the Targa Florio.

ing of the CSI in March 1968 the smaller constructors put this point most strongly. In April 1968 the CSI issued another rule, which brought down the number of cars necessary to classify as 'production' to 25.

This was a number that Porsche, following their custom to sell one-race (or a-few-races-only) cars to customers, could cope with. And while the 3-liter 908s could hold their own, if Ferrari decided to go for a run of 5-liter cars they would sweep the board. And, as with the 908, and the 907 before that, and the 910, they had most of the building blocks for a new model already. In June 1968 the go-ahead was given.

Porsche often make the claim that they are in the forefront of technology.

There have been times when this is so – they were among the leaders when it came to mid-engined racing cars. But on the whole their thinking is very often conservative. The 917, spectacular to drive though it is, was not a revolutionary design.

It retained, for example, a multi-tubular space frame, admittedly made from aluminum, but by the late 1960s almost all other manufacturers were producing machines based on monocoques, as in the Ford GT40s for example. The suspension was by conventional coil springs and wishbones – though it must be admitted again that this is still *de rigeur* wear for all forms of racing car.

Left, right and below right: The combination of Gulf sponsorship, John Wyer teamwork and the Porsche 917 in Gulf's blue and orange colors was one of the most successful in sports car racing in the early 1970s. All those shown here are short-tailed K (for *Kurz*) versions.

The fact that time was short could well be a very good reason for this conservatism, especially if the car was to be ready for Le Mans in 1969. Thus the engine had to be air cooled: they knew about such things at Zuffenhausen. Naturally, too, it had to be a boxer.

The simple solution was to add yet another four cylinders to the 908's 3-liter flat eight. Instead of shafts and bevels to operate the valves, gears would be used, driven by one large central gear on the crankshaft dividing the engine into two six-cylinder units. One unusual feature was that the drive to the transmission was via a shaft geared to this central gearwheel as well, instead of from one end of the crankshaft. The rest of the engine – heads, valves, cylinders and so on – drew on Porsche experience. Thus there were only two valves per cylinder, again at a time when four was becoming fashionable. The body shape drew strongly (for the initial cars anyway) on the 908L. Conservative, evolutionary, call it what you will, a car weighing as little as 1760lbs, with a capacity of 4494cc and 540bhp, which is what the first engines gave, would be something else indeed.

The first anyone outside Porsche (and the members of the FIA responsible for homologation) knew about the 917 was at the Geneva Motor Show which opened on 13 March 1969. Finished in plain white, with a green flash across the nose, and Shell, Dunlop and Cibie stickers on it, there was a 917 on Porsche's stand.

The FIA, realizing that a very large and powerful machine was about to drive through their loophole, wouldn't accept the partly completed cars and piles of components as proof that 25 necessary cars would be ready by 31 March at their first inspection on 20 March.

When the representatives of the CSI arrived for their second inspection on 21 April, they saw something that must have shaken them to the core: there, neatly lined up, were 25 identical white 917s!

Like the 907Ls, those early 917s were hard to drive. Vic Elford recalls:

'I fell in love with the 917 right away – it was my sort of car. The first testing we did was at Spa, Jo Siffert and I drove it, and came in and said the same thing: it's going to be great, but not yet. It was undriveable – along the Masta straight you couldn't keep it flat because it used all the road. Frightened us silly . . . Fortunately for Mitter, who was due to drive it in the race, it broke half-way round the first lap . . .

My next race (though not the car's) was Le Mans, and I asked for a 917 because I liked it so much. Bott said there was no point, it would only last eight hours, but eventually I persuaded him to let me have one.

I had Richard Attwood as co-driver, and at the end of 21 hours we were 80kms in the lead – then an oil seal let go.

But we'd proved the point. The car was unbelievably fast, and had a fiercesome reputation among other drivers – they'd only have to see us in the mirrors and they'd queue up on the right to let us past! Mind you, the handling at the end of the Mulsanne straight was terrible. You couldn't go off the accelerator on to the brakes. You had to lift off gently, then brake gently, otherwise the back would take over from the front. We even had to lift off for the kink in the Mulsanne straight, yet the next year we were going through there at 230mph, flat, in the rain, and the following year we were doing 240 . . .'

The first year of 917 life, 1969, was really a shake-down period while all the problems, mainly aerodynamic, were overcome. The costs of the 917 program were enormous, and the number of valuable people working on it was also considerable. Thus it was that during 1969 Porsche approached John Wyer informally to discuss the possibility of the JW concern taking over the running of the 917s. Porsche, JW and Gulf met, discussed the matter, and in September 1969 announced that JW would bear responsibility for the organization and running of the Gulf-Porsche team as it would be known. Porsche would supply the cars and provide the JW team with the latest technology.

Somewhat to John Wyer's astonishment, not to say annoyance, shortly thereafter it was announced that Porsche-Salzburg, Louise Piëch's organization, would field a team of 917s as well! However the Gulf-Porsches had direct access to the experimental department while Porsche-Salzburg would have to rely on the racing service department. Still, competition from within 'the family' could not have been particularly welcome.

The collaboration had in fact started before the official announcement of the Gulf-Porsche tie-up had been made. Both Porsche and JW had raced at the Osterreichring, and afterwards put their heads together during a test session to sort out the 917's unpredictable handling. Also there was Porsche's first Spyder version of the 917, the 917PA, named after the Porsche + Audi American connection: it was being tried out as a possible Can-Am contender.

It was little more than a 917K with the roof lopped off and a simple body which swept up gently to a lip right at the tail, which was sharply cut-off.

The results were dramatic: the drivers took to the 917PA immediately. It was rapidly realized that it was the aerodynamics of the 917's tail that were wrong. There and then, with the aid of tinsnips, sheets of aluminum, and trial and error, the bodywork was crudely modified – but worked.

Thus for 1971 the 917K was homologated with a new body. A more blunt, concave nose was used, and the rear wings were modified to a 917PA-type profile, rising to the rear with adjustable flaps at their ends for fine trimming.

The first appearance of the new shape was at Daytona late in January 1970. Gulf entered two cars, Porsche-Salzburg one. The Gulf cars finished 1-2, driven by Rodriguez/Kinnunen and Siffert/Redman, the P-S car retiring.

However, a few weeks later at Sebring everything seemed to go wrong – in particular new front hubs of an advanced design which sidelined both Gulf cars. Andretti's Ferrari won, with Steve McQueen's and Peter Revson's 908 Spyder second.

From there on, though, life became glorious. At Brands Hatch, in April, 917s filled the top three positions. At Monza, where one of the cars was fitted with a 4.9-liter engine for the first time, a 4.5-liter Gulf car won. At Spa, Siffert and Redman took the honors with the P-S car driven by Elford and Ahrens third, bracketing the Ickx/Surtees Ferrari – the Modena make couldn't be dismissed *that* easily.

But Le Mans was the big prize, and Porsche and its teams brought out the big guns. During the earlier part of the year Porsche had been working with

the internationally recognized Paris-based SERA wind tunnel establishment. They had designed a new long tail for the 917Ls. It was taken to the Le Mans trials in April and compared with an original 917L and a 917K. The K was quickest – or at least gave the drivers most confidence – and so Wyer chose Ks for his onslaught.

Thus Gulf lined up three 917Ks for Le Mans: two with 4.9-liter engines, and one with a 4.5-liter.

Two 917Ls were entered, one by P-S to be driven by Elford/Ahrens with a 4.9 engine, the other, finished in an astonishing color scheme of purple with green whorls, by Martini with a 4.5 engine to be driven by Larrousse and Kauhsen. Backing up the P-S car was a 917K with Hans Herrmann and Englishman Dickie Attwood behind the wheel.

Neither of the Gulf cars nor the P-S 917L survived, but the Herrmann/ Attwood car soldiered on to win, after which Herrmann, having won the race in which he had entered 14 times, and come so close to winning the year before, promptly retired from racing! In second place was the garishly finished Martini car.

The team of Rodriguez and Kinnunen won at both Monza and Watkins Glen for Gulf, while Siffert and Redman took the last race in the World Championship of Makes, again for Gulf, in Austria in October. Porsche had won the Championship, and after Zeltweg Porsche-Salzburg sold out to Martini.

The next year, 1971, the 917s steam-rollered the opposition out of sight. They won at Daytona and Sebring with 4.9-liter 917Ks, and at Monza with the 5.0-liter (actually 4999cc, just within the limit) version.

The Le Mans test weekend in April showed that at last the 917Ls had handling to match their speed. Gulf entered two Ls, as did Martini, all with 4.9 engines. One of the latter's machines was the oddest 917 ever. It was a SERA design of vast width, so much so that the tires looked quite lost within the bodywork. Tony Lapine's styling studio, who had been responsible for the color scheme of the purple and green car the year before, poked gentle fun at the shape: they painted it pink then applied dotted lines as per a butcher's diagram of the relevant cuts of a pig. Naturally the car was dubbed the 'Pink Pig'!

To his regret, John Wyer's Gulf team missed out on the honors again, the Martini car of Marko and van Lennep cantering home first from the 13th hour, keeping a reasonable gap between them and the Gulf car driven by Attwood and Muller which was second.

The rules for the World Championship of makes changed for 1972, as Porsche had known all along they would. The 5-liter limit had only been given

a brief life simply to give the GT40s and Lolas and the other American-engined cars an extended period of competitiveness. The fact that Porsche had seen the loophole and had reacted so quickly could not have been foreseen by any others than those at Stuttgart.

But the best was yet to come. The 917s may have been outdated in Europe and the World Championship of Makes, but over in America there was a racing series, the Can-Am, that was capturing everyone's imagination. It was for two seater sports/racers, but there was no limitation on engine capacity or a minimum weight. It was almost a case of 'anything goes.' The regular winners were Lolas and especially the Chevrolet-powered McLarens, with massive 7- and 8-liter engines. The racing was spectacular, to say the least. Could the 917s be developed in another direction?

With the creation of the Porsche + Audi operation Stateside, P + A pressed Stuttgart for a Can-Am machine to get the new set up an instant image. Porsche mounted a toe-in-the-water exercise in 1969, based on the 917 that had appeared that day at Austria when it was realized that the 917's aerodynamics were all wrong.

The 917PA was named in honor of the American company. The first one, basically just an open 917 – a Spyder in Porsche parlance – was very smooth indeed, from its low, long, slippery nose to its abbreviated tail.

Porsche had spent so much time on the 917Ls during 1969 that the 917PA was late arriving on the Can-Am scene. The driver was Jo Siffert, the man in charge Ritchie Ginther. The car was given the odd number 0!

Using a 4.5-liter engine, the car didn't do too badly, though it was fairly soon apparent that, though the aerodynamics were better than the 917 coupes, they weren't too brilliant either. It sprouted huge spoilers either side of the front wings, which were vulnerable in knock-about competition, so a new design of nose was invented. With an underpowered, barely developed car, the 917PA nevertheless gave Siffert an overall fourth in the Championship. It was promising.

Porsche backed out of Can-Am in 1970, concentrating on the manufacturers championship, but late that year the logical decision to follow the Can-Am trail, starting in 1972 when the 917's career elsewhere would be almost over, was taken.

During the winter of 1970 a new design, designated the 917/10, was put in hand. The car was based on the 917 chassis and running gear, but a new body was designed for it. Very wide to cover the fat tires, it had elements of the 917PA and 908 in its design.

To match the horsepower of the American engines, Porsche first of all en-

larged the flat twelve to 5374cc, which gave about 660bhp, but at the same time started work on a much more engaging scheme: turbocharging.

By the time the Can-Am series started in 1971, Porsche were far from ready (as they knew they would be) but gave Siffert a 917/10 chassis equipped with a 5-liter engine, to make a solo foray into a series he loved. He obtained some sponsorship from Marlboro and STP but was basically paying much of the cost from his own pocket. He was showing some good placings when he was unfortunately killed in a horrifying accident in England. That was the end of the Can-Am trail for 1971.

For 1972, Porsche wanted someone to run the team in America, along the lines of the Gulf-JW and Martini arrangement. They chose Roger Penske Racing, whose Sunoco-backed Ferrari 512 had given the 917s a run for their money at times. Porsche and Penske parried during the middle of 1971, but on 16 November it was formally announced that the two would combine to contest the 1972 Can-Am series. Their arsenal was to be the 917/10.

Penske's driver, Mark Donohue, was also a brilliant sorter of cars – and he was impressed with Porsche, and the use they made of Weissach. It was a mutual admiration society, for the Porsche engineers, from Ernst Fuhrmann, who replaced Ferdinand Piëch in October 1971 following the famous family withdrawal, on down held Donohue in the highest esteem.

Donohue stayed over in Germany, testing the 917/10, for weeks. The first car, fitted with an unblown 5-liter engine, was sent to America in December 1971 for testing on the American tracks. It proved disappointingly slow.

While Donohue spent much of the early part traveling to and from Germany, development was being carried out at Zuffenhausen on two fronts. The first was turbocharging: a 4.5-liter blown unit was sent to America in January 1972: it developed 800+bhp. But it was undriveable, the throttle acting more like an electric switch than a proper accelerator. This problem

was sorted out through tinkering with the fuel injection system, which worked to Donohue's satisfaction. So the Porsche engineers promptly applied their turbochargers to a 5-liter engine, with sensational results – flash readings of 1000bhp were seen on the dynamometer!

The second front was to the running gear and body. Tests at Weissach had shown that a 100 percent locked differential gave the best handling, so the differential was deleted. A new nose was developed, whose fenders were S-shaped with a flat tray nearest the ground: between them the oil cooler was mounted in a boxy-looking structure. At the back a huge wing was supported by massive fins.

The first outing of the Penske 917/10 was at Mosport on 11 June. A little fault caused a pit stop, which slowed Donohue down and he finished second. Then, in practice for the Road Atlanta event, the rear deck came off and Donohue had a massive accident, the car destroying itself and putting Donohue in hospital. George Folmer took his place in the team, and drove splendidly – so well, in fact, that he won five races in the series to Donohue's one after his return to the track, and thus took the Can-Am Championship title for 1972.

There were other 917/10s made that year, some for Can-Am, though only the Penske team had the 5-liter blown engines all the time – the others used unblown 5.4-liter units to start with but were gradually upgraded to 4.5-liter blown, then 5.0-liter blown units by the end of the season. Leo Kinnunen won the Interserie championship in a 917/10.

How to begin to describe that final, last, glorious year for the 917? Penske and his team had two brand new cars to play with. They were completely redesigned, from their SERA-inspired nose, thicker and more voluptuous than that of the 917/10, to its long tail, adapted from the late 917Ls. It was longer yet slightly narrower, and the truly enormous rear wing was carried by long, long fins. With its stunning finish, in dark blue with red and yellow flashes, it looked like what it was: the most powerful racing car for road circuits the world had ever seen. The engine was a turbocharged 5.4-liter, and delivered a regular 1100bhp, though outputs up to 1500bhp and more were seen on the dynamometer.

The first two races of the 1973 Can-Am series saw other cars win, both 917/10s: an accident in the first race and a fuel leak in the second were not good omens for the 917/30. But from then on nothing could even begin to come near to Donohue: he won six races in the series and the Championship.

After that, both Donohue and Porsche announced retirements, the former from racing (though he did return to race in Formula 1, only to be tragically killed) and Porsche from Can-Am. The rules had been changed, so often the case when one marque is seen to dominate so completely, and the 917/30s were out of contention.

Every so often the racing world throws up truly magnificent machinery, such as the pre-War Mercedes-Benz and Auto Unions: and there is a direct line from those Auto Unions to the 917/30, the car that was the pinnacle of all that Porsche stood for.

Left: The original 917/10 test hack, photographed during tests at Weissach, when the standard superb finish was of lesser importance!

Above: The view out of the panoramic windshield of the 917 was quite something, but sideways and backwards – well, who needed it? Nothing except another 917 was going to come past.

Right: The ugly duckling test hack seen on the left was turned into this ugly duckling but immaculate racer by the time it appeared on the circuits of North America.

Domination on the Tracks

Previous pages: Sportscar racing of the 1980s summarized in one picture – a Rothmans-sponsored Porsche 956 with Jackie Ickx at the wheel. The combination dominated the scene as never before.

Left: Back to racing with identifiable cars, the 911 and its derivatives. Ickx flies at Silverstone in 1976 in the early version of the 935 with headlamps in the standard position.

Below right: Forerunner of the 934s and 935s, the 1974 Carrera RSR Turbo – second overall at Le Mans was its best result.

1973 marks the fourth watershed year in Porsche's competition history. Life in the upper echelons of the company must have been at times exhilarating and inspiring, at times depressing and disheartening. The traumatic withdrawal of the family from an active part in the business, and the poor sales in 1971, were counterbalanced by the tremendous efforts of the fabulous 917s on the track.

When Dr Ernst Fuhrmann took over in late 1971, he must have taken a long hard look at the workings of the company, and tried to map out its future. There was at least one fairly inescapable conclusion: prestigious the 917s may have been, but the racing program was taking up too much time, effort and cost.

But his thinking went deeper than that. Did Porsche owners identify with the 917s? They were as far removed from reality as you could get. Would it not be better to develop the 911 into a machine that would not only win races and rallies, but which looked like a production car as well?

Thus this fourth period in the story of Porsche and competitions could be subtitled 'The 911 and its derivatives.'

Almost from its beginning in 1964, the 911 had been entered in competitions. Its initial successes came in rallying, with such famous drivers as Sobieslav Zasada, Vic Elford, Pauli Toivonen and Bjorn Waldegard giving them some fine victories, including three Monte Carlo rallies in a row and the European Rally Drivers' Championship in 1968 and 1970.

And, gradually too, the 911 began to appear as winners in the GT category of motor racing, at such venues as Le Mans, the Nurburgring and the Targa Florio. There was, in the 911, a firm foundation on which to build.

Fuhrmann's first step was to authorize, in May 1972, the development of a 911 variant that could begin to take on the Ferraris and other large GT cars that held sway. To do this a number of things would be required: more power, for a start; less weight for another; and improved roadholding and handling for a third.

The Carrera RS 2.7 was the result. Weight was pared to a minimum, the engine capacity was increased to 2.7 liters to compete in the 3-liter class, and wider tires under bulging wheelarches were fitted. The rules then governing the GT category allowed various modifications to be made for competition, such as even wider wheelarches and fatter tires and the extraction of yet more power. Thus was born the Carrera RSR.

The engine capacity was increased to 2806cc, which, with other modifications such as twin plug heads, gave a healthy 300bhp at 8000rpm. The oil cooler was fitted in a hole where the license plate usually goes, right in the nose. Nine-inch front and 11-inch rear wheels were standard thanks to the extra 2 inches of wheelarch width allowed, and assorted other suspension changes lowered the car and gave it tremendous roadholding.

In fact the first RSR victory came before the RS had even been homologated. It was at Daytona in February 1973, and the homologation papers for the RS didn't come into effect until 1 March. Even more astonishing was that the RSR, running as it had to in the prototype class, won overall. A battle royal developed during the race between the Penske team of Donohue and Follmer, who were to dominate the Can-Am series that year, and the Brumos Porsche car driven by Peter Gregg and Hurley Haywood, victory going eventually to the latter pair.

The 1973 works team, Martini-backed, consisted of two cars entered mainly for races counting towards the World Championship of makes. To give RSR customers a more sporting chance, one of the cars was modified way beyond what the rules allowed and thus competed in the prototype class. It won another famous international race outright, the last of the Targa Florios on the Little Madonie circuit. The other car ran in Group 4 races. Lessons learnt on the track were filtered through the racing services department to RSR customers.

The prototype Carrera raced by the factory had a full 3-liter (actually 2994cc) engine. This used a stronger aluminum crankcase instead of one made from magnesium.

The RSR would surely be a winner with the 3-liter engine, but how to homologate it? The answer was relatively simple: the Carrera RS had been built in such quantities (about 1600) that it qualified for Group 3, a normal production car. An evolution of the model only required 100 to be built – so Porsche built 109 Carrera RS3.0s, thus qualifying them for Group 3 for the 1974 season, with the racing version, the RSR, falling into Group 4.

The latter car had even bigger bulges around the fatter (10.5-inch front, 14-inch rear) wheels. The front fenders were widened all the way back to the leading edge of the door and there was an air duct in the front of the rear fender. The engine, in the same state of tune as the prototype from the year before, gave some 330bhp.

The company did not race any of the RSR3.0s, leaving that to their customers. And they repaid Porsche's confidence: in 1974 they won the IMSA Championship, the European GT Championship, the FIA GT Cup and a whole list of other major GT successes – then went on to repeat the same performances again in 1975.

Porsche declared that they would enter a Turbo Carrera in group 5 in the World Championship of Makes in 1974. This set an upper limit of 3 liters unblown, which reduced by a factor of 1.4 if a turbocharger was used. The cars would face a full complement of out-and-out racers such as the Matras, Alfas and Mirages. But there were also rumors that, as from 1975 or 1976, the World Championship of Makes would be for Group 5 production-based cars – something that would suit Porsche admirably.

Thus the 2.14-liter Turbo Carrera came into being. The odd capacity comes from the 1.4 equivalence factor.

The drivers during 1974 were Herbert Muller and Gijs van Lennepp, and their best result was a second place at Le Mans. They achieved the same position at Watkins Glen, were third at Spa, fifth at Monza, sixth at the Nurburgring, and seventh at Paul Ricard. These were fine results for a car that, although ultra-light and producing 450bhp (give or take a few depending on boost pressure) was still under the skin a production car.

There were no works Porsches in 1975, since the new regulations had indeed been announced for the 1976 season. They included Groups 3 (Production Touring Cars), 4 (Limited Production GT Cars), and 5, which was in fact the class for the World Championship of Makes. This group (5) more or less encompassed Groups 1 to 4 but with considerable modifications allowed and a minimum weight based on a sliding scale depending on engine capacity, while the basic bodyshell, the major castings and their location, the general layout and the type of suspension had to be standard. Group 6 was for Prototypes.

Porsche attacked on three fronts – Groups 4, 5 and 6.

For Group 4, the 934 was created. The name is significant, since it indicates that it is based on the Type 930, for Group 4, the same applies for their other new models, the 935 and the 936.

The 934, with the blown 3-liter engine, had an imaginary capacity of 4.2 liters when the turbocharger equivalency rule came into play. To bring it up to the minimum weight limit it was barely stripped at all – even the electric windows were left in place! There was a reinforcing bar between the MacPherson strut suspension towers and an x-shaped cross brace above the luggage space. It was fitted with BBS 16-inch wheels.

The 934 had its share of success in the 1976 season, winning the Trans-Am Championship with George Follmer and the European GT Championship with Toine Hezemans.

Porsches second string to their bow was to become one of the most famous racing cars in the history of the sport. It was the immortal 935.

Porsche drew on their experience with the 2.14-liter Turbo Carrera of 1974. To keep below the effective 4-liter class, and therefore the weight

down, a capacity of 2856cc was chosen: the claimed power output was 590bhp at 7900rpm, using a mechanical fuel injection pump.

The nose was filled with a vast petrol tank, and aluminum strengthening tubes as used in the 934 stiffened the nose area. Coil springs replaced the torsion bars all round, and there was a rear anti-roll bar which could be adjusted by the driver from the cockpit. The brakes were developed from those of the 917. The whole car, of course, was lightened quite considerably – so much so, in fact, that ballast was required to make it legal. Most of the non-structure panels were made from a fiberglass/polyurethane sandwich: these included the doors, engine cover, and the whole front section including both fenders and the front spoiler/valance.

The first 935s featured massive rear wings, again supported on a box structure which also held the air-air intercooler, but at a race at Imola, this was decreed out of order by the scrutineers, so Porsche had to revert to water-air intercoolers, their radiators housed in the space in the rear fenders.

After a couple of races, too, the front fenders were modified in a way that the rule makers had most definitely *not* intended, but which was quite within the letter of the law. The regulations stated that fenders were free – they could be any size or shape. The intention was to allow wide flares, but Porsche took the FIA at their word – and chopped off the whole of the headlamp/fender top on each side. This gave better penetration and more downforce at the front, plus better stability in sidewinds. The headlamps were incorporated into the front spoiler. The rule makers didn't like it, but they had to accept it!

The initial hassles over the inter-cooler, and the problems associated with the water-cooled system, took Porsche a while to overcome. Eventually, though, four victories, three seconds and three thirds plus a fifth, with Ickx and Mass doing most of the driving, gave Porsche the World Champion of Makes title for 1976.

Meanwhile, the third string to their bow was doing equally well. The Group 6 championship for 1976 was suddenly wide open when Alfa Romeo withdrew, leaving Renault, almost by default, as far and away the most likely winners.

Fuhrmann made his decision: Porsche would go Group 6 racing as well.

Left: Occasionally someone else would try and compete with the 935s – in this case BMW – but without a great deal of success.

Below left: Porsche-only races are popular throughout the world – this is one such, for the Pirelli Challenge, in England, with 911s as far as the eye can see.

Right: Brands Hatch 1977, and the 936s fight it out among themselves.

Below: The T-Bird Swap Shop 935 K3 spits flames out of its tail on the over-run, a characteristic of turbocharged cars and especially the 911-derived models with their short exhaust pipes.

Left: In 1978 a Porsche didn't win Le Mans; this one, driven by Ickx, Wollek and Barth, came home second.

Below left: Ickx and the 936 were still at it in 1981, this time with Derek Bell and Jules sponsorship, to win Le Mans yet again.

Right: As the 935 was developed, the aerodynamics changed dramatically. Compare this shot of Bob Wollek at Silverstone in 1977 with that of Ickx on page 100.

Below: Porsche took advantage of a loophole in the regulations to carve the headlamps off the top of the fenders for the later 935s, and thus changed the face of racing.

The go-ahead was given in September 1975, and the first car was being tested in February 1976.

The 936 combined the 917 with the 2.14-liter turbo engine. The space frame was longer and lower, but the 917 background was quite evident. Even the transaxles came from the 917. The 2.14-liter engine was chosen for the same reason as in 1974: the equivalency factor put it in the 3-liter class.

Porsche entered two 936s in 1976, sponsored by Martini, for the World Sports Car Championship. During secret testing before any racing was carried out the car was finished in a matt black color as a 'disguise,' though it fooled no one. However, Count Rossi, of Martini and Rossi, liked it, and for its first race at the Nürburgring it appeared in black but with the Martini stripes. However his color scheme didn't show up too well on the television cameras, so was abandoned from then on.

That Nürburgring race was the only one the 936 didn't win. For Le Mans a huge air intake/cooling scoop was installed behind and above the driver's head – but what needed cooling was his feet. With the low chassis the drivers sat much closer to assorted radiators with devastating results to their feet. Nevertheless the inevitable happened, and Ickx and van Lennep won.

Three were made, and again they walked over everything in sight – and if they didn't the customer 935/76s did (a small batch had been made for sale at the end of 1976, just as a batch of 935/77s would be at the end of 1977). Once again Ickx and Mass were the major drivers, and yet again Porsche won the World Championship of Makes. By now Porsche were in an overkill situation. They so dominated those classes in which they were entered that racing began to look like a one-make affair.

For 1977 Porsche decided not to race the 936 except in one race, *the* race – Le Mans. Detailed refinements were made to the bodywork, and twin KKK turbochargers were fitted to the 2.14-liter engine. Two cars were entered, both 1976 models with the 1977 treatment. One retired, and Ickx transferred to the other which, due to a faulty injection pump, was lying way back. Slowly the remaining car worked its way up the leader board, and when the leading Renault dropped out, Ickx and Barth were in front. And then, with less than an hour to go, a piston holed. The third driver, at the wheel at the time, was Hurley Haywood: he brought the car in. Such was the lead at this point however, that the car still won in spite of having to complete the last couple of laps under its own power on five cylinders.

For 1978, Norbert Singer produced another surprise. He took advantage of the rules and removed the whole floor pan of the 935 replacing it with an aluminum tube cross-bracing frame and a fiberglass floor. This had the effect of lowering the car by no less than three inches. The nose and rear body sections were replaced by a tubular structure. With its extended nose and tail, on which sat a wing supported by triangular fins, the whole car looked decidedly weird, and was promptly nicknamed 'Moby Dick!'

In the early stages of development Singer tried the idea of joining the front and rear wings so that the sides were fully enclosed. Unfortunately the CSI wasn't going to wear this one, but eventually a compromise was reached: the front wings could extend half way back along the doors.

The most significant change, though, was to the engine. There had been growing signs that the 911-based cylinder heads were near the limit as far as performance with reliability were concerned. In addition, four valves per cylinder offered scope for yet more power.

Thus a new engine was designed. The crankshaft and crankcase remained those of the 930 Turbo, and the cylinders were still air-cooled, but new, water-cooled four valve heads were grafted on.

The new engine was laid down with three capacities: 3211cc for Group 5,

Left: The first major body changes to the works 935s came in 1976 with the sloping nose to give much more downforce – and the rule-makers a fit.

Below left: Ickx tripped up in 1980, and, with Jöst, could only manage a second place at Le Mans.

Right: Tire test day at Le Mans, 1978, the year the 936s were defeated by the Renault Alpine of Jaussaud and Pironi. You can't win 'em all.

Below: Derek Bell brought Autoglass (a replacement windshield company) sponsorship with him when he raced a 962 at Brands in 1987.

2140cc for Group 6, and 2650cc for potential use at Indianapolis. The last engine never actually appeared at Indy, since the officials insisted on a boost rating too low to give the engine a chance. The 3.2-liter capacity was chosen for the 935/78 Moby Dick car to give it maximum power and hence top speed at Le Mans. With 750bhp this was achieved, the car being immensely quick down the Mulsanne straight, but what seemed to be a serious oil leak (later found to be relatively minor) relegated it to eighth position.

Porsche's second Le Mans string for 1978 were the 936/78s. These were basically the 1977 cars but fitted with the 2.1-liter versions of the four valve water cooled head engines. Two of these were entered, along with the 1976 winner brought up to 1977 specification. One of the 2.1-liter cars crashed, the other retired, and the older car finished third. A Renault won.

In 1979, the works Porsches were limited to two of the 936s with 2.1-liter engines as of the year before. Renault had pulled out of sports car racing to concentrate on Formula 1, and the rest of the Group 6 field did not look all that strong. So at the last minute, with Essex sponsorship, Porsche entered the 936s. As expected, they dominated the early hours of the race, but the Ickx/Redman car was seriously delayed after a tire blew, and was then disqualified for receiving outside assistance. Later the Wollek/Haywood car went out with a serious misfire.

In spite of which, Porsches overwhelmed the opposition. Three 935s took first, second and third, with a 934 fourth! The winner was a Kremer-prepared car driven by Klaus Ludwig and the Whittington brothers, with another Kremer car third, while second slot was filled by the Dick Barbour car, driven by Dick himself, Rolf Stommelen, and 54-year-old film star Paul Newman.

This win, along with literally hundreds of others throughout 1979, showed how much the private teams contributed to Porsches successes over the years, and how the 935s were all but unbeatable, works cars or otherwise. That year saw the 935's fourth successive win in the World Championship of Makes. Of the teams running 935s, the two that stand out are those of Kremer and Loos. The former preferred to develop their own cars, the latter relying rather more on factory advice.

In 1980, Porsche left racing to the privateers on the whole, with no works 935s, or 936s. However, the 1979 Frankfurt Show had seen the return of a famous Porsche name – the 924 Carrera. Porsche made no secret that this was an homologation special and announced a production run of 400 cars. In standard form it produced 210bhp

To show the potential of this machine, a team of three were entered for Le Mans in June 1980. These were effectively out-and-out racers developing 320hp thanks to (in part) an increase inboost from 0.7 bar to 1.3 bar. As they had to run in the prototype category, almost anything went. One finished sixth, the other two 12th and 13th.

For 1981, the World Championship of Makes rules were altered, and the 3-liter limit was no longer enforced, while the IMSA American formula – basically Group 5 with detail differences – was becoming an important part of the racing scene. Thus the line-up for Le Mans saw no less than 19 Porsches out of the 55 entries – and probably the widest variety of the marque for many years. In the GTP (GT Prototype) class there was a Porsche 924 Carrera GTR, but it was no secret that the engine under the bonnet was not based on the Audi unit but on Porsche's up-coming 944. It was a 420bhp full race engine featuring twin overhead camshafts, four valves per cylinder, and a turbocharger. In Group 6 there were two more special Porsches, these being 936s fitted with the aborted 2560cc Indy engine modified to run on gasoline, but still producing some 600bhp even with low boost for long distance racing. There was also a 917, believe it or not, and Reinhold Jöst's venerable 908.

The race was a walk-over for the Ickx/Bell 936, which won by the enormous margin of 14 laps. Rondeaus filled the next two places, but a Kremer K3 935 finished fourth. The Rohrl/Barth 944 Prototype came in seventh. Neither the 917 nor the 908 lasted the distance, both being out by the seventh hour.

And so to 1982, for which FISA introduced a new category, Group C. This replaced the old Group 5 as the class around which the World Endurance Championship of Makes was based, and the 3-liter Group 6. Emphasis was placed on efficiency by restricting the amount of fuel a car could carry to 100 liters, and limiting the number of refueling stops a car can make in a given race. The hope, too, was that speeds would be limited.

Porsche jumped at the formula – they had been making excellent (at times

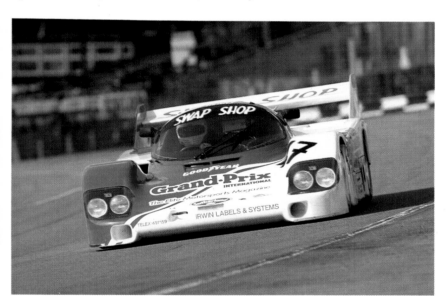

Above left: Appropriately numbered, this 956 is the third place finisher of Haywood and Holbert at Le Mans in 1982, behind two others.

Left: One of the more successful private entrants was GTI Engineering with Cannon support, who could attract such notable drivers as Jan Lammers and Jonathan Palmer, seen here at Brands Hatch in 1983.

Above: A rare one-off drive in the Preston Henn 956 for the talented lady racer Davina Galica at Brands Hatch in 1983.

Right: No works Porsches at Le Mans in 1984, but a 956 won anyway, the Jöst-entered car driven by Pescarolo and Ludwig, despite being 30th at one point.

Above: It's all over in 1987 and the flag marshalls greet the winner.

Left: Of course a Porsche would win Le Mans in 1985, but to almost everyone's surprise, except the winners', it was the same Jöst 956 as the year before.

Right: Porsche's new weapon for 1985 was the 962 – it may not have won at Le Mans but it gave Bell and Stuck the joint Drivers' Championship at the end of the year.

spectacular) progress in improving their production car economy, and this was a way of showing the direction in which they felt motor racing really should develop.

For the new formula, Porsche designed a (for them) radically new car. For a start it was the first racing Porsche to feature a monocoque chassis. The engine was the 2.6 Indy unit, which the Porsche engineers had worked over in the interests of better economy. At it's first outing at the now-traditional Silverstone 6 Hour meeting, in order simply to keep going, it was necessary to run at a slow pace. But the 956C, as the car was called, showed promise.

Backing up the three 956Cs of the factory at Le Mans were two more Category C Porsche-powered cars: one was a spaceframe car, powered by the 2.1-liter engine from Reinhold Jöst, the other an all-new car from Kremer, the C82. This used a 2.8-liter 935 engine, and featured the Kremer's own monocoque chassis.

The result is now history. For this, the 50th anniversary of the 24 hour race at the Sarthe circuit, Jacki Ickx, partnered by Derek Bell, won his sixth victory, and the 956s finished first, second and third. Two 935s followed them home, giving Porsche one of their best years ever. Not only that, but with three outright wins, Porsche finished up at the end of the year as the Champion of Makes, and Ickx the Driver's Champion.

Like the 917s, 936s *et al*, the 956 came to dominate the world of long-distance sports car racing. For 1983 the basic Group C rules were kept, and an attempt was made to enrole the Americans into the game. They had their own series, run by IMSA, with similar but not *quite* the same regulations. One, for example, required the driver's feet to be behind the front axle line, in the interests of safety. Over the years attempts have been made to amalgamate the two, but – to date – without success.

In the great scheme of things, 1983 cannot be called a vintage year. The only opposition to the works, Rothmans-backed cars, the 956/83s, were the undoubtedly fast but equally undoubtedly fragile Lancias. The 956/83 was very much an updated 1982 car, lighter, revised aerodynamically, and, most important of all, kitted out with an electronic engine management system. In addition, Porsche built 12 customer cars to the 1982 spec (no electronics). In fact, it was just one of these, entered by Jöst, which won the first race of the year, at Monza, much to Porsche's chagrin.

Some all-night work at Weissach proved highly effective, however, and from then on the Rothmans-Porsches swept everything aside, taking another six races. One of them – of course! – was Le Mans, but towards the end there was some comic drama. The drivers were Al Holbert, Vern Schuppan and Hurley Haywood, who had a most comfortable lead. Then, in the last stint,

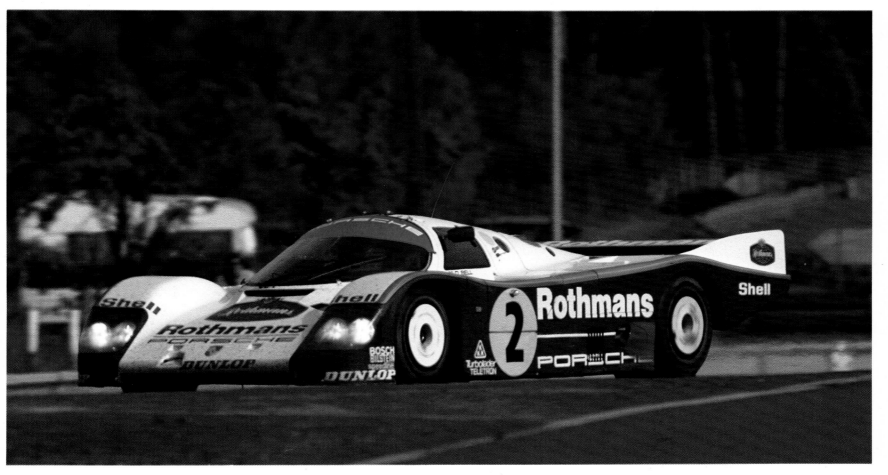

Above: Porsche so dominated Group C in the mid-80s, as here at the Nürburgring in 1984, that the Championship was changed from one for makes to one for teams.

Left: The dynamic duo, Ickx and Bell, cruised to an uneventful Le Mans win in 1982 ahead of two more Rothmans 956s.

with Holbert driving, the engine over-heated and he completed the last lap in near hysteria with no water at all! The famous Ickx/Bell team were second and in all nine 956s finished in the top ten. Now that's domination. The year's end results tell it all: Porsche won the Makes Championship by 100 points to Lancia's 32, and Ickx just edged out Bell to take the Driver's Championship.

The works Rothmans-Porsche team cruised through 1984, again using basically the 1982/83 cars but with an even more efficient engine manage-ment system – and an ingenious semi-automatic gearbox, the PDK unit, which used electronically-controlled twin clutches to give near-instant, full-power changes. It wasn't *always* reliable. In addition, the privateers, such as Jöst, GTI/Cannon, Brun, Fitzpatrick and Kremer were carrying out their own developments on chassis and aerodynamics to some considerable success. This after an initial early-season programming fault in the customer elec-tronic ignition system leading to a series of 16 (expensive) engine failures.

A row erupted early in the year when FISA – forever the bane of Porsche's existence – introduced a fundamental rule change, reducing the fuel allow-ance by 15 percent in yet another attempt to bring the Americans in (they still preferred their own system of a sliding scale of weights and engine capac-ities) and Porsche, in a fit of pique, withdrew the works cars from Le Mans. It really was a bit of a hollow gesture, since all the teams were out in force, and it was a foregone conclusion that a 956 would win. What wasn't a foregone conclusion was that it would be the Jöst car that would win, for the first few hours were a disaster, and at one point it was dead last! However, long-term Le Mans exponents Henri Pescarolo (three previous wins) and Klaus Ludwig (one) slowly worked their way back again, and when it was all over they were in front. The overall results weren't as good as the previous year, though: 956s only filled eight of the top ten places.

The sensation of the year had been the German driver Stefan Bellof, who was at the wheel six times out of the seven races the works cars won, thus taking the Driver's Championship – and naturally Porsche won the Makes Championship.

Porsche, meanwhile, had developed a variant of the 956 for the IMSA Championship, the 962, late in 1983 and early in 1984. It was, in fact, almost a brand-new car: there was a 4¾in longer wheelbase, for example, so that the driver's foot rule could be met, which meant a new monocoque and fuel cell, modified aerodynamics, and a considerably altered engine bay, since IMSA rules only allowed one (big) turbocharger for the 2.85-liter, two-valve, single-plug engine. The ubiquitous Derek Bell and Al Holbert campaigned throughout 1984 in the IMSA series and although winning five times had to give second best to series winners Lanier and Whittington in a March-Chevrolet.

For the 1985 season, therefore, Porsche concentrated their development on the 962, which – for Group C – became the 962C. The major change was the use of the 4-valve, twin-turbo powerplant (giving over 640bhp!) in place of the single-turbo unit, and taller rear tires for a better 'venturi effect' at the tail.

As before, the '15 percent fuel reduction' rule caused major headaches, and many races were run – and lost – at low speeds as drivers strove to con-serve their fuel. Those who could balance speed with economy usually won, and this was never more apparent than at Le Mans. That a Porsche would win was never in doubt once again, but the winning car, crewed by Ludwig, Paolo Barilla and 'John Winter,' was the same Jöst-entered machine (chassis number 956/117) that had won the year before.

Just to finish the 956 story, yet more rule changes meant that 1985 was its

Left: Le Mans 1986, with 962s and 956s as far as the eye can see – but among them is the challenge of the future in the form of the Jaguars and Saubers.

Below: The Bell/Stuck/Holbert 962 held off the Jaguars for a win in 1986 – Bell for the fourth time, Holbert the second, and Stuck for his first.

Right: Smart pit-work for the 1986 winner – the gent climbing all over the car is simply cleaning the windshield.

last competitive year, for it would be obsolete by 1986. But look at its record: between 1982 and 1986 it won 27 Makes and Driver's Championship races. That's more than the 917 – indeed, more than any other Porsche except the 935, which won 38. The 956 was very much in the Porsche racing tradition: fast, reliable, and a winner. The only trouble was that, with so little opposition, racing tended to be between the teams, rather than between makes, and if you weren't a Porsche fanatic it could all be a little boring. Nevertheless, that doesn't stop the 956 being a classic.

The first part of the 1985 season was spent trying to sort out the electronics on the engine management system so that the works cars could be driven both quickly and economically. But it wasn't until after Le Mans that this nut was cracked and the Rothmans-Porsches started winning by achievement rather than default. However, 1985 will also be the year than many at Porsche would rather forget. At Hockenheim an explosion of the fuel tank in the pits left team manager Norbert Singer badly burnt; at Mosport, Manfred Winkelhock crashed fatally, and at Spa, Derek Bell and Stefan Bellof tangled and the brilliant and popular German lost his life. Some consolation was that, at last, the British driver and Hans Stuck were declared the joint Drivers' Champions.

Until 1986, Porsches had totally dominated the World Championship of Makes, so much so that it was renamed the World Championship of Teams! But, in 1984, a glimmer of opposition appeared on the horizon. First, Jaguar announced their return to sports car racing, with V12 power and the strength of Tom Walkinshaw's operation to build the cars and run them. Second, the small Swiss team Sauber started running a Mercedes-Benz powered car – and it eventually became clear that the other Stuttgart company was more than just an interested onlooker. The engines in the Saubers came from the factory of the three-pointed star.

Thus 1986 saw the Rothmans-Porsches (and, of course, the other Porsche teams) with some real opposition. However, the Jaguars and Saubers were still on their learning curve, while the 1986 962C was a known quantity. The works soldiered on with the troublesome (and heavy) PDK gearbox except for Le Mans, where a standard box was installed in two of the three cars. The race was marred by Jo Gartner's terrible accident in the Kremer 962, and this slowed the pace for a good couple of hours while the wreckage was cleared away. The ensuing slow running put out the famous Jöst 956, 956/117, winner of the previous two Le Mans and going for a third, so that Bell, Stuck and Holbert ambled round with an eight-lap lead to win in the works non-PDK car.

Although Porsches won the majority of WEC races in 1986, Jaguar took

Left and below left: The Jaguar challenge at the Sarthe was much, much stronger in 1987. But at the end of the day the Bell/Holbert/Stuck Porsche 962C outlasted them all for a repeat win of the year before.

Right: Defeat at last at Le Mans for the 962 in 1988 – but it was an honorable defeat, for the Bell/Stuck/Ludwig red and yellow Dunlop-sponsored car harried the winners right to the end.

Below: Meanwhile, lesser mortals could take their road-going Porsches out to play, such as this 2.7 Carrera in the Porsche Club of Great Britain's Pirelli Championship.

then on, and at the end of the year Porsche were third in the Championship behind Jaguar and Brun, with Bell fifth in the driver's classification. Mind you, there were still five Porsche-based teams in the top six.

But Porsche couldn't resist one more shot at Le Mans, and for 1988 produced a superb team numbering Stuck, Bell, Ludwig, and the Andrettis father and son in the team. Subtle modifications included the latest Bosch Motronic 1.7 engine management system for the engine, which had been fully water cooled since 1986. The results show that a Jaguar won, but they don't show just how close it was, for the Stuck/Bell/Ludwig car harried the leaders from start to finish: it was, in effect, a 24-hour sprint race, and the Porsche was only 2½ minutes behind the Jaguar at the end. It was a fitting swan-song for a car which, remember, had been basically designed back in 1982.

In America, too, the 962 had been enormously successful, and, what's more, against strong opposition. Customers included Bruce Levin, Preston Henn, the legendary A J Foyt, and Al Holbert, whose Lowenbrau-backed cars formed a quasi-works team. Up against them were the Jaguars again, first via Bob Tullius' Group 44 team and then Tom Walkinshaw's TWR efforts: Chevrolet with the Lola chassised Corvette GTP; Ford with the Probe, and Nissan with Electramotive, not to mention all the March and Lola based, American-engined, 'specials.' In spite of this, the Porsches, up until 1988, were the cars to race – and win. Between 1984 and the end of the 1987, they were beaten only 11 times, and scooped the checkered flag no less than 46 times. Sadly, Al Holbert, in charge of Porsche's North American racing operations, was killed in an aircraft crash in mid-1988, and the company lost not only a brilliant organizer and long-distance driver but a good friend as well.

If Porsche's efforts in endurance racing seemed to be fading as the 1980s progressed, there was a good reason for this: they became involved in other forms of the sport, and time and personnel were limited. The most important form of the sport was the ultimate – Formula 1.

Back in 1977 Renault appeared on the scene with an 'alternative' engine, a turbocharged, 1½-liter. At first it didn't seem much of a threat to the 3-liter Cosworth V8, but by the early 1980s it was clear that turbocharged engines were the way to the future. Users of the Cosworth searched around for alternative suppliers: Brabham, for example, found BMW.

McLaren's Ron Dennis approached Porsche in 1981. Would they, he asked, be willing to build engines for F1? Much to almost everybody's surprise, Porsche said yes – but on condition that McLaren found the money to pay for the whole operation. Porsche, in effect, looked on it as another

the Silverstone event and Sauber the Nürburgring (where both works 962s were destroyed.) Thereafter it was a Jaguar/Porsche battle all the way to the line, and the end results depended on the last race at Fuji. The organizers placed the Warwick/Cheever Jaguar in second place, and, by the points scoring system, this meant that Jaguar won the Team Championship and Warwick the Drivers'. It wasn't until three weeks later that it was announced that, after a check on lap charts, the Jaguar had finished third. This gave the Team Championship to Brun, and the Drivers' to Bell.

Coming into 1987 the 962s were showing their age. Although down to the weight limit, the Porsche engineers had wrung what they could out of the old sheet aluminum monocoque instead of starting afresh with a more rigid composite structure. It was unquestionably a Jaguar year, the Coventry marque winning every round of the Championship except two. One of the ones they didn't win was – Le Mans! The organizers provided a strange witches brew instead of fuel, and this played havoc with all the Porsche teams, while the Jaguars had their problems, too. The surviving works 962 was hastily fitted with a revised chip in the Motronic engine management system and Messrs Bell, Stuck and Holbert ran strongly to finish first by a huge margin. It was an historic win: Porsche's seventh in a row, Bell's fifth, Holbert's third, and Stuck's second. Just after this, Porsche dropped a bombshell when it was announced that they were cutting down on endurance racing, due to pressure of other work. As in days gone by it was left to the privateers from

Left: The total all-round car – you could drive your Porsche on the road, enter it in races, or take it on the Monte Carlo rally such as here in 1974.

Below: Others experimented with their own version of Porsche's 956 and 962, usually without success. One such was the Kremer brothers' CK5.

Right: Imola 1986 and the McLaren-TAG team of Rosberg and Prost play tag. Prost finished second and went on to a World Championship.

customer project, such as designing a new car for SEAT in Spain. Dennis found a suitable sponsor in the form of the Arabian Mansour Ojjeh's company *Techniques d'Avant Garde*, or TAG for short – Porsche were into Formula 1.

The engine was a gem, a little 1½-liter (91-cu in), 80 degree V6, which, fitted with twin KKK turbochargers and a Bosch Motronic engine managememt system, was capable of giving 650bhp plus, revving to 12,000rpm. Power alone was not enough, though. Just as in endurance racing, the powers that be had decided that the cars were getting too fast. So they used the same ploy to slow things down and began to limit fuel capacities. Thus the engines had to be powerful *and efficient*. In this, of course, Porsche excelled.

The new engine was ready for the 1983 season, but that year was really spent sorting things out. Matters all came together in 1984, and the superb engine, McLaren's unmatched design and organizational abilities, and the

talents of two of the greatest drivers the world has ever known, Niki Lauda and Alain Prost, saw a clean sweep. Between them the two drivers took 12 out of 16 rounds that formed the F1 season. In fact, they were the only two in contention – and there was no quarter given between them. The Championship went right down to the line and in the last race, at Estoril in Portugal, Prost won but Lauda finished second, and in doing so eventually took the Championship.

The next year, 1985, life was more difficult. Williams in particular, caused the McLarens problems. Their Honda engines were giving indisputably more power than the Porsche-TAG units, and in the hands of Nigel Mansell and Keke Rosberg they pulled off four wins. The dazzling, but erratic, Ayrton Senna took three – but, at the end of the year, the wily and cool Alain Prost emerged as Champion, with five wins out of McLaren's six. Yet again the strength of the Porsche-TAG engine had been its efficiency, balancing fuel consumption against horsepower.

Left: Two of the many well-known Porsche drivers were Bob Wollek and Stephan Johansson, the latter becoming a works Ferrari F1 star: here he conducts the Jöst 956 at Brands Hatch in 1983.

Below left: Star of the McLaren-TAG firmament, Alain Prost leads the 1985 Monaco GP which he went on to win.

Right: With a capacity the same as the average family saloon, only 1500cc, the Porsche-designed TAG engine could deliver over 650bhp.

Below: One of the most successful of Porsche racing activities has been the Porsche Turbo Cup Challenge, a one-make series based on the 944 Turbo – this is the Avus round in 1988.

Above and left: In 1986 the Porsche 959 driven by Rene Metge and Dominique Lemoyne won the Paris-Dakar. But if this scenery looks odd for such an event that's because Porsche let Scottish rallyman Jimmy McRae loose in one in England for an *Autocar* feature.

Above and below right: The career of the racing version of the 959, the Type 961, was brief, with a seventh (and the only GTX entrant) here at Le Mans in 1986 and a retirement the next year.

In 1984, the fuel tank limit had been 220 liters, for 1986 it would come down to 195 liters – this was highly unpopular, especially with the drivers. 'Driving with one eye on the road and the other on the fuel gauge is not my way to go racing,' said Prost.

There was a driver shuffle at the beginning of 1986: Lauda retired for the second time, so Rosberg joined Prost at McLaren, while Nelson Piquet took his place at Williams. If the Porsche-TAG engine had been the top of the class in 1985, by 1986 the Honda was clearly superior in terms not only of power but of reliability and economy as well. It was under these conditions that Prost proved himself the greatest driver in the world: his consistency gave him the Championship by two points, with four outright victories (compared to Nigel Mansell's five, for example). Williams, however, took the Constructor's Cup by a massive margin. At the end of the year, the FIA announced that, starting in 1989, turbos would be banned, and that F1 would be run to a 3.5-liter, naturally aspirated, formula.

Over the winter of 1986/87 the Porsche engineers worked hard on the TAG engine, and at the beginning of 1987 it had been much improved. But then development stagnated – the Porsche-TAG contract ended at the end of the year – and, for once, reliability became a problem. Just little things, but enough. Of more significance, Honda worked continuously on their engines, and it showed. Piquet and Mansell in their Williams dominated as the McLarens had done in 1984, and there was nothing anyone else could do about it. Except Prost: he only finished fourth in the Championship, but in the process won three *Grandes Epreuves*, while McLaren came second in the Constructor's Cup again. At the end of the year, the Porsche-TAG engine was retired, and Williams turned to Honda.

Meanwhile, as if the Porsche engineers didn't have enough to do between 1981 and 1987 with the Group C and Formula 1 efforts, the launch of the 959, in September 1983, indicated that the company was branching out yet again, into what appeared to be a potentially strong area: Group B. This called for a limited run of 200 cars, ostensibly production based (in silhouette, at least), for both rallying and racing. This, of course, was Porsche meat and drink, as displayed by such machines as the 934 and 935, and Audi had shown, via stunning successes in rallying with their quattro, what could be done. But the times changed too quickly for the 959 (and its racing

derivative, the 961). Loopholes in the rules in effect led to ultra-lightweight, mid-engined, super-powerful forest racers such as the Peugeot 205 Turbo 16, the Lancia Delta S4, and the Ford RS200, and the 959 rally car was obsolete before it began. In addition, the whole Group B scene was abolished in 1986.

There was, though, one event which ran to its own rules, the toughest in the world: the mad, bad, Paris-Dakar Raid. Jacky persuaded Porsche that they should enter, and in 1984 there were three Porsches in Rothman's colors. They weren't 959s, since they stuck with 3-liter engines, but they did have mechanical 4-wheel drive. The Frenchman Rene Metge won in one of these hybrids, with Jacky Ickx sixth after suffering a burnt-out wiring loom. Back they came in 1985, with machines nearer the 959, but with unblown 3.2-liter engines in the interests of reliability. All retired, however, Ickx and Mass through hitting rocks, and Metge missing a time control.

Thus it wasn't until 1986 that the definitive 959s appeared in this crazy, 8700-mile race through the Sahara, and this time there were no mistakes. Metge had no serious problems and came home a clear winner – by nearly two hours – ahead of Ickx in second place. What's more, the back-up crew finished sixth.

That was the end of the 959s rallying career, but not quite the end of the story. A 959 was turned into a 961 racer, much lightened and power boosted to 640bhp, for Le Mans in 1986. Apart from a burst tire, it cruised its way home to seventh overall. The next race was at Daytona, where tire problems meant it finished a lowly 24th overall. It was hauled out once more, for Le Mans 1987, but was actually slower than the previous year, and eventually crashed. And that really was the end of the 959 saga: so much promise, so little accomplished.

On a trip to Weissach in late 1987, I was shown around the competitions department. Downstairs were a couple of 962s, ex-Le Mans, sitting idle. Upstairs in one corner a couple of TAG engines were being fettled – but one of those was being turned into a display unit for Mansour Ojjeh. It might have been a sad little scene – except that over on the other side of this clinically immaculate workshop there was considerable bustle around yet another engine. It was a water-cooled V8, of 2.7-liter capacity, and with a single Garrett turbocharger. On the test bed it had already shown 750bhp (though we didn't know that until later). It represented yet another break with Porsche tradition, for it was intended to go into a single-seater for a series of races held exclusively in North America, those organized by CART (the Championship Auto Racing Teams). They were immensely popular in the States, the rules were stable, and – above all – they included in the series the Indy 500.

Now Americans, it is said, only know two races: Le Mans and the Indy 500. Porsche had, for sure, made their mark at the Sarthe circuit: they were now turning to the American classic. After all, was not America their major export market?

Breaking with Porsche tradition the new car was called simply the 2708 – no Project 9-- here – and was to be built completely by Porsche, their first single-seater since 1962. The first example, with sponsorship from Quaker State, was rushed to completion in time to start at Monterey in October 1987 – where it proved to be sadly slow. A failure even to qualify at Miami made the point. The problem was not a lack of power but the chassis, and for 1988 the company relented and used March chassis. To date success has eluded the 2708, and the death of Al Holbert was a particular blow. We shall just have to wait and see.

Where now for Porsche in the competition field? A clue may be found in the enormously popular Porsche Turbo Cup series for 944 Turbos: how about a Porsche 911 Speedster series? Then there's the Indy car (2708) project still on the go. The rules for International motor racing are going to be based on a standard engine, 3.5-liters naturally aspirated, for both Formula 1 *and* endurance racing. Can Porsche afford to keep out of this potentially far-reaching formula? Ask those who know, and the only reply you get is an enigmatic smile. But the idea that Porsche *won't* be in international competition is quite unthinkable.

Left: The way to the future? Porsche's major involvement in motor racing in 1988 and 1989 is in CART racing with the 2708.

Below left: Soldiering on, or 911s never die – the Richard Sutton-prepared SCRS 911 Turbo contested the 1984 European Rally Championship with moderate success.

Right: The CART car's 2.7-liter, water-cooled, turbocharged V8 giving some 750bhp.

Below: Success has so far eluded the March-chassised 2708, even though it looks magnificent.

Appendix

1948 Type 356 Prototype
Tubular chassis, mid-engined
Flat 4, 1131cc, 40bhp
Wheelbase: 84.6in
Number made: 1

1950-1954 Type 356
Platform chassis, rear-engined
Flat 4, 1086cc, 40bhp (1950-1953)
Flat 4, 1286cc, 44bhp (Normal),
60bhp (Super)
Flat 4, 1488cc, 55bhp (Normal),
70bhp (Super)
Wheelbase: 82.7in
Number made: 7627

1955-1959 Type 356A
Platform chassis, rear-engined
Flat 4, 1286cc, 44bhp (Normal),
60bhp (Super)
Flat 4, 1488cc, 55bhp (Normal),
70bhp (Super)
Flat 4, 1582cc, 60bhp (Normal),
75bhp (Super)
Flat 4, 1498cc, 4 camshaft
100-110bhp (Carrera)
Flat 4, 1587.5cc, 4 camshaft,
105-115bhp (Carrera)
Wheelbase: 82.7in
Number made: 21,045

1959-1963 Type 356B
platform chassis, rear-engined
Flat 4, 1582cc, 60bhp (Normal),
75bhp (Super), 90bhp (Super 90)
Flat 4, 1966cc, 4 camshaft,
130bhp
(Carrera)
Wheelbase: 82.7in
Number made: 30,963

1963-1965 Type 356C
Platform chassis, rear-engined
Flat 4, 1582cc, 75bhp (C), 95bhp
(SC)
Flat 4, 1966cc, 130bhp
Wheelbase: 82.7in
Number made: 16,668

1964-1969 Type 911 2 liter
Monocoque chassis, rear-engined,
Coupe or Targa
Flat 6, 1991cc, 130bhp (911),
160bhp (911S), 110bhp (911T),
140bhp (911E), 170bhp (911S
1968-1969)
Wheelbase: 87in (to 1968), 89.4in
thereon

1969-1971 Type 911 2.2 liter
Monocoque chassis, rear-engined,
Coupe or Targa
Flat 6, 2195cc, 125bhp (911T),
155bhp (911E), 180bhp (911S)
Wheelbase: 89.4in

1971-1973 Type 911 2.4 liter
Monocoque chassis, rear-engined,
Coupe or Targa
Flat 6, 2341cc, 130bhp (911T),
165bhp (911E), 190bhp (911S)
Wheelbase: 89.4in

1971-1977 Type 911 2.7 liter
Monocoque chassis, rear-engined,
Coupe or Targa
Flat 6, 2687cc, 210bhp (Carrera
2.7),
150bhp (911), 175 (911S),
Wheelbase: 89.4in

1975 to date Type 911 3.0 liter
Monocoque chassis, rear-engined,
Coupe, Targa or Drophead
Flat 6, 2994cc, 200bhp (Carrera 3),
165bhp (911S), 180bhp (911SC)
Wheelbase: 89.4in
Number made: still in production

1965-1968, 1975 Type 912
Monocoque chassis, rear-engined,
Coupe or Targa
Flat 4, 1582cc, 90bhp (1965-
1968),
1971cc, 90bhp (1975)
Wheelbase: 87in then 89.4in
Number made: 30,300 (1965-
1968),
2099 (1975)

1975 to date Type 911 Turbo
(Type 930)
Monocoque chassis, rear-engined,
Coupe
Flat 6, 2993cc, turbocharged,
260bhp
(1975-1977), 3299cc, 300bhp
(1977 to date)
Wheelbase: 89.4in
Number made: still in production

1969-1971 Type 914/6
Monocoque chassis, mid-engined,
removable roof
Flat 6, 1991cc, 110bhp
Wheelbase: 96.5in
Number made: 3360

1976 to date Type 924
Monocoque, front-engined, rear
wheel drive, Coupe
Straight 4, water-cooled, 1984cc,
125bhp (924), 177bhp (924 Turbo)
Wheelbase: 94.5in
Number made: still in production

1978 to date Type 928
Monocoque, front-engined, rear
wheel
drive, Coupe
V8, water cooled, 4474cc,
240bhp
V8, water cooled, 4664cc,
300bhp
(928S)
Wheelbase: 98.4in
Number made: still in profuction

1981 to date Type 944
Monocoque, front-engined, rear
wheel
drive, Coupe
Slant 4, water cooled, 2479cc,
163bhp
Wheelbase: 94.5in
Number made: still in production

RACING

1953-1956 Type 550
Ladder frame, mid-engined,
Spyder
Ladder framed, mid-engined,
Spyder and Coupe (1956 space
frame Type 550A)
Flat 4, 1488cc, 78bhp
Flat 4, 4 camshaft, 1498cc,
110-130bhp

**1956-1963 Type 718 RSK/RS60/
W-RS**
Space frame, mid-engined, Spyder
and Coupe
Flat 4, 1587cc, 150bhp
Flat 4, 1697cc, 165bhp
Flat 4, 1966cc, 165bhp
Flat 8, 1982cc, 210bhp

1959-1061 Type 718/2
Formula 2/Formula 1
Space frame, mid-engined, single
seater
Flat 4, 1498cc, 155bhp

1962 Type 804 Formula 1
Space frame, mid-engined, single
seater
Flat 8, 1494cc, 180bhp

**1964-1966 Type 904 Carrera
GTS**
Ladder box-section chassis,
glassfiber
body bonded on
Flat 4, 1966cc, 180bhp

1966 Type 906 Carrera 6
Space frame, Coupe
Flat 6, 1991cc, 210bhp

1967-1968 Type 910
Space frame, Coupe and Spyder
Flat 6, 1991cc, 220bhp
Flat 8, 2196cc, 270bhp

1967-1968 Type 907
Space frame, Coupe and Spyder
Flat 6, 1991cc, 220bhp
Flat 8, 2196cc, 270bhp

1969-1971 Type 908
Space frame, Coupe and Spyder
Flat 8, 2997cc, 350bhp

1969-1973 Type 917
Space frame, Coupe and Spyder
Flat 12, 4494cc, 580bhp
Flat 12, 4905cc, 600bhp
Flat 12, 4998cc, 630bhp
Flat 12, 5374cc, 660bhp
Flat 12, turbocharged, 4494cc,
850bhp
Flat 12, turbocharged, 4998cc,
100bhp
Flat 12, turbocharged, 5374cc,
1100bhp

1976 Type 934
Monocoque, production based,
Group 4
Flat 6, 2994cc, 330bhp

1976 Type 935
Monocoque, production based,
Group 5
Flat 6, 2856cc, 590bhp
Flat 6, 2856cc, 630bhp (935/77)
Flat 6, 1425cc, 370bhp (935(2.0)
Flat 6, 3211cc, 750bhp (935/78)

1976-1981 Type 936
Space frame, Spyder, Group 6
Flat 6, 2143cc, 520bhp
Flat 6, 2143cc, 540bhp (936/77)
Flat 6, 2140cc, 580bhp (936/78)
Flat 6, 2560cc, 600bhp (936/81)

1982-1985 Type 956
Monocoque, coupe
Flat 6, 2560cc, 600bhp+

1985-1988 Type 962C
Flat 6, 2994cc, 640bhp+

Index

Acknowledgments

The publisher would like to thank
David Eldred the designer, Maria
Costantino the picture researcher,
Emma Callery for editorial assistance
and Ron Watson for compiling the
index. Special thanks to Porsche Cars
(Great Britain) Ltd., and Porsche Cars,
Stuttgart, West Germany for their help
with the photographs. The individuals
and agencies listed below kindly
provided the illustrations

Bison Picture Library: pages 71,
90(below), photos: Nicky Wright:
25(below), 37(below), 54(below),
60(top), 61.
Jeff Bloxham: pages 103(top),
112(below), 117(top), 120(below).
Neill Bruce Photographic: pages
18-19, 22(top), 26(top), 27(top),
30-31, 37(top), 38(both), 41(top),
42-43, 46(bottom 2), 49(all 3),
52(below), 77(top), 85(top).
**Neill Bruce/Midland Motor
Museum, Bridgnorth:** page 95(top).
Neill Bruce/Photo: Peter Roberts:
page 118-top).
Phil Drackett: page 8(below).
**Haymarket Publishing/Photos:
Michael C. Brown:** pages 124(top),
125(below) / Graham Gould: page
29(top) / Doug Nye: page 96 /
Oblinger: pages 13(top), 14(top),
20(top), 77(below), 95(below), 101 /
Jeremy Shaw: page 125(top).
Haymarket Publishing/Autocar:
pages 9(below), 20(below), 21(both),
26(below), 34(top), 40(below), 45(top

2), 50-51, 53, 54(top), 55(both),
59(top), 64(top & right below), 65,
66(both), 67(all 3), 68(both), 74-75,
84, 88, 89(below), 102(top), 104(top),
105(top), 106(top), 107(top), 108(top),
109(below), 112(top), 121(both).
Haymarket Publishing/Autosport:
pages 76(top), 79, 80(below), 83,
85(below), 89(top), 90(top), 92(top),
93(both), 97(both), 100, 110(both),
111, 114(both), 115, 116(both), 119,
122(both), 123(both).
**Haymarket Publishing/Classic and
Sportscar:** page 11(top).
Andrew Morland: pages 33(top),
52(top), 58, 63, 82, 86-87, 91.
Don Morley: pages 36(below), 98-99,
108(below), 109(top), 118(below),
120(top), 124(below).
National Motor Museum, Beaulieu:
pages 23, 29(below), 40(top), 47, 48,
56-57, 62(both), 64(below left),
70(below), 72(below), 73(below).
**National Motor Museum, Beaulieu/
Nicky Wright:** pages 24, 27(below),
35, 80(top), 92(top).
Porsche Cars: pages 6-7, 8(top),
9(top), 10(both), 11(below), 12(below),
14(below), 15, 16, 17(both), 28, 32,
33(below), 34(below), 36(top), 39,
41(below), 44(both), 45(below),
59(below), 60(top), 70(top),
72(top), 73(below), 76(below),
78(both), 94, 104(below), 105(below),
106(top).
Mike Walsh: pages 12(top),
22(below), 81, 92(below).
Stuart Windsor: pages 25(top),
102(below), 107(below), 117(below).